Heritage Sites in the Borders

John Dent and Rory McDonald

Scottish Borders Council
Economic Development and Environmental Planning

© Scottish Borders Council
Council Headquarters
Newtown St. Boswells
MELROSE
Scottish Borders
TD6 0SA

A British Library Cataloguing-in-Publication Data record for this book is available from the British Library

ISBN: 0 9530438 4 3

Designed by the Graphics Section
Scottish Borders Council
Printed and bound by Kelso Graphics, The Knowes, Kelso, Scotland, TD5 7BH

First Published 2001
Economic Development and Environmental Planning, Scottish Borders Council
Related Website: www.scottishbordersheritage.co.uk

Foreword

All the customer research carried out in developing a vision for the Scottish Borders as Scotland's Leading Short Break Destination has underlined the importance of the area's history and rich cultural heritage as key selling points in attracting visitors to the region.

It is one matter being aware that we have both in abundance: It is another task altogether presenting this information in a way that will both educate and excite people to want to visit and experience the area's pride and passion at first hand.

By identifying, cataloguing and describing over 170 of the Borders heritage sites and publishing them in this attractive guide, the authors have achieved just that. They are to be commended too for the way that so many of the descriptions tell a human, as well as a physical, story.

This of course is not a guide produced solely for visitors. Many local residents will, I am sure, enjoy expanding their knowledge of the area, finding more information about sites they knew existed and discovering many more that are uncovered in the pages of this guide for the first time.

All of the sites listed in this publication have one common link and that is they exist and are significant because of the involvement of people. People who conceived and designed them, people who built them or described them, people who lived and worked within them.

I hope that all who read the pages that follow will likewise be inspired by the legacy left to them by people who came before and conserve our rich heritage for generations to come.

Riddell Graham
Chief Executive
Scottish Borders Tourist Board

Acknowledgements

This book was written, compiled and edited by John Dent and Rory McDonald of the Archaeology and Countryside Section, and designed by the Graphics Section of Scottish Borders Council, as part of the "Heritage Interpretation Project".

Scottish Borders Council is pleased to acknowledge financial support from the European Regional Development Fund and Scottish Natural Heritage which assisted in the production of this book.

We would like to thank the following people for their help and advice during the preparation of this book: Chris Badenoch, Mark Douglas, Steve Hunt, Ian King, Keith Robeson, Scottish Borders Council Museum and Galleries Service, Scottish Borders Tourist Board.

Introduction

The historic counties of Berwickshire, Roxburghshire, Selkirkshire and Peeblesshire make up most of the Scottish Borders area, which today is perhaps best known for its scenery, textiles, rugby, fishing and associations with Sir Walter Scott. Visitors remark on the friendliness of the people, the wide scope for walks or rides through beautiful countryside and the romance of historic ruins. The peace and quiet that the Borders offer today has not always been so. Historically the region lay between the English counties of Northumberland and Cumberland to the south, and Dumfriesshire and the Lothians on the Scottish side. Castles, towers, forts, and places with such names as "Bloody Bush" or "Skirmish Field" are reminders that the border between Scotland and England was a dangerous place to live. However, the heritage of the Borders consists of much more than the remains of those violent years, important though they are to the traditions and sense of being of present day Borderers.

The ancient rocks that make up the region have a story of their own, which can be read not only in old quarries and the coastal cliffs, but in the very stones which make up most of the buildings in the region. The conditions under which these rocks formed have more in common with California or Indonesia than they do with most other parts of Britain.

Although the abundant natural heritage is to be valued and enjoyed throughout the Borders it is not the focus of this book, which looks at the places where, over the past ten thousand years, people have lived, worked and died. A wholly natural landscape has not existed in the region since settlers re-colonised the area after the last Ice Age and immediately began to make their mark by cutting down trees, establishing camps and lighting fires. Gradual clearance of natural tree cover, the cultivation of land and the construction of settlements, burial mounds, boundaries and roads started the process by which people came to shape and dominate the landscape. Although the Borders has a rich diversity of plants and animals, the hand of man is apparent everywhere and the whole landscape is managed to a greater or lesser degree.

This diversity of species and the outstanding landscapes which they inhabit are as rich as the Highlands. Along the spectacular Berwickshire coast, which includes the highest cliffs on the East Coast of Scotland, it is possible to catch glimpses of many species, including the Puffin and Harbour Porpoise. The lowland areas of the Borders are made up of a series of small valleys (hummels) and low ridges (knowes). Wetland areas, such as mosses which were once the haunt of reivers and moss-troopers also survive, a relic of vast marshes left by the melting glaciers. The majority of these were drained during the Agricultural Revolution but the remainder provide an important habitat for species such as Reed Bunting, Black-necked Grebe and Lapwing. Woodlands shelter Red Squirrel and Roe Deer, while lochs and reservoirs attract wintering wildfowl such as Greylag and Pink-Footed Geese, sometimes by the thousand. The uplands are home to Juniper, Grouse, Merlin and Curlew, which is known locally as "Whaup". Central to the life of the Borders is the River Tweed and its tributaries which provided routes for the first settlers to travel deep into the regions and begin the processes which shaped the landscape of today. In recent centuries these rivers provided the basis for the power behind the textile mills of the Industrial Revolution and subsequent growth of the Borders' towns. Today the Tweed is one of the major Atlantic Salmon rivers in north-west Europe and supports populations of creatures such as the elusive Otter and the Kingfisher.

This and other books in the Heritage Series are intended to draw the attention of visitors and residents alike to the significance of the historic landscape and to places where it can be enjoyed. Places listed are simply a selection of accessible historic sites, which in some cases provide additional interest in the form of natural history, architecture, literature or the visual arts. Sites are grouped by settlement, except for some rural locations where the commonly used name is more convenient. All are located by National Grid reference for use with Ordnance Survey maps, of which a range exists at various scales for the Borders. Landranger 1:50,000 scale maps are recommended, although more detail appears on 1:25,000 scale maps of the Pathfinder and Outdoor Leisure Series.

Please remember, whenever visiting these sites, in normal circumstances always follow the Country Code:

- Guard against all risk of fire
- Fasten all gates
- Keep dogs under close control
- Keep to paths across farmland
- Avoid damaging fences
- Leave no litter
- Safeguard water supplies
- Protect wildlife, wild plants and trees
- Go carefully on country roads
- Respect the life of the countryside

Table of Contents

Background to the Borders

Background to the Borders

The Southern Uplands are the ancient rock barrier that separates Edinburgh, Glasgow and the central valley of Scotland from the counties of Northern England. The eastern block of these uplands is drained by the River Tweed and has long been known as "The Borders". Here, like a horseshoe, the hills wrap around the low-lying Merse, through which the Tweed runs its final course to the North Sea. To the south is the Cheviot and to the north the Lammermuirs, while to the west the massif gradually rises towards the Dumfries and Galloway border and to the height of Broad Law at 840 metres (2,756ft).

These border hills are the result of a long geological history which began in the Southern Hemisphere around 500 million years ago as part of the slow collision of two tectonic plates. Similar processes are still continuing, and their effects can be seen, along the western seaboard of the United States and in the southwest Pacific. The oldest rocks, known as shales and "greywackes" were sediments on the floor of a shrinking ocean. Much later the layers were squeezed and contorted into corrugations that can still be seen in road cuttings and derelict quarries, particularly in the western Borders and the Lammermuir Hills. Some of these, for example at Innerleithen, show signs of ancient Ice Ages. Later sediments were bedded sandstones and shales, and these were sometimes reddened by the iron minerals they contained. The "Old Red Sandstone" was laid down around 370 million years ago and has been widely used as *freestone* in building, particularly in the north-eastern Borders. In the Merse and along parts of Liddesdale Carboniferous Sandstones and poor limestones were laid down more than 300 million years ago. These honey-coloured rocks were also for used for building and are the basis of the fertile soils of the Merse.

Prominent outcrops of volcanic rocks, such as at the Eildon Hills, St Abbs Head, the Dunion and Black Hill of Earlston, punctuate the rolling hills and ridges produced by these sediments. The former volcanoes and the lava outflow known as the "Kelso Trapps" consist of very hard basic crystalline rocks. Where they have been used in field dykes and house walls they usually appear as black boulders.

Two million years ago the Ice Ages began and continued up to about 12,000 years ago. The land cooled and glaciers formed in the hills, bulldozed their way across the landscape mostly in a south-west to north-easterly direction and scattered rock debris when they eventually melted. Gravel eskers, clay drumlins and deep meltwater channels, particularly around West Linton, Yetholm, Innerleithen and the Merse between Swinton and Duns are relics of this arctic phase of the Borders climate.

As temperatures gradually rose again, the landscape was colonised, firstly by hardy, low-growing plants and later by trees and the insects, birds and animals which fed on them. By 6,000 years ago the landscape was almost completely covered with trees and shrubs and peopled by bands of hunter-gatherers who moved about the country in search of food. Ironically, at about this time the long process began by which the woodland eventually disappeared.

A 5,000-year-old hunting bow was found near St Mary's Loch in 1991. This may have belonged to someone who ate only wild foods that he had caught or collected, or it could have been lost by an early farmer. The knowledge of cereal cultivation originated in the east and was brought into Britain along with domesticated sheep, pottery and more effective stone tools. Cultivation formed the basis of permanent settlements and steady population growth and ultimately led to disappearance of the natural tree cover from the landscape. The oldest built monuments in the Borders were constructed at an early stage in this clearance process. Burial mounds and large ceremonial monuments were designed for open landscapes in which they were readily visible from a distance.

Knowledge of metalworking arrived in the 3rd millennium BC and 2,000 years later gold, silver, copper, tin, lead and iron were all being used to produce an ever-widening range of ornaments and tools, including some of exceptionally fine quality. Wheeled vehicles were also in use, implying tracks or roads capable of carrying them, and hundreds of hill forts and homesteads, sometimes separated by earthwork land boundaries, testify to a much larger population. The need to feed these extra mouths required new arable areas, which were created by clearing more trees.

The development of these early British tribes and their social organisations, economies and environments was arrested by the invasion of northern Britain by the Roman army in c.79BC and subsequent annexation of the Southern Uplands by the Roman Empire. By this stage, there is evidence that some woodlands were coppiced as a source of fuel, although the demand for building timber continued to use up standard trees, and grazing animals prevented their regrowth in many places. The lasting monument of this phase was Dere Street, a strategic road which extended as far as York and which retained its importance long after the military posts had been abandoned.

The break up of Roman Britain into petty kingdoms based upon tribal groupings was complicated by invasion by settlers from Ireland (*Scotti*) and the North European Plain *(Angli)*. Only as these groups gained ascendancy over the native tribes, and the kingdoms of Scotland and England began to emerge, did the issue of a border arise.

Anglian place names in the eastern Borders date from the time when lower Tweeddale and Teviotdale were part of the kingdom of *Northumbria*, while native British and intrusive Irish names in the hills to the west indicate where the Angli failed to penetrate. The part played by Dere Street and the North Sea in this cultural change is demonstrated by the focus they formed for early Christian communities at such places as Old Melrose, Jedburgh and St Abbs Head.

The introduction of Christianity from the south followed earlier missionary work by Ninian, based in Galloway, but occurred at about the same time as the community at Iona in Argyll was extending its influence over northern Britain. Early monasteries were ill equipped to deal with violence when it came, and Old Melrose and St Abbs monastery were put to the torch, the latter by the Vikings in the 9th century.

By 1018 the lower Tweed had become the accepted frontier between Scotland and England and the region became a true borderland. Norman culture and institutions swamped England after 1066 and inspired Scottish kings to introduce them north of the border. In the 12th century King David I in particular granted land to Normans, endowed monasteries and established trading burghs as centres of local government.

A religious revival in the 11th and 12th centuries was represented in the Borders by the establishment of churches in each parish to serve the spiritual needs of the community, and by the endowment of monasteries. Four major abbeys and several lesser houses were established as communities of religious devotees. These houses were maintained largely by gifts and other incomes derived from agriculture and certain rights to church revenues. The medieval church had a virtual monopoly of literacy and learning, so priests were especially valued as scribes and lawyers.

Normans brought with them the feudal system, of which the lasting symbol was the castle. Families such as the Balliols, Bruces and Riddells took their names from places in France but also had lands in England. Other landowners took their names from their chief residence in the Borders, such as Gordon, Home and Maxwell. Maxwell ("Maccus' Well") and Maxton ("Maccus' Town") were named after Maccus, an early 12th century landowner of Anglo-Scandinavian origin. The medieval kings relied on such families to uphold law and order in the Borders.

The establishment of local government was closely linked to the development of regional economy through foreign trade. Royal Burghs were established at Berwick, Roxburgh, Selkirk and Peebles with trading monopolies administered by a Council of Burghers. Each was dominated by a royal castle where a Sheriff appointed by the king attended to the king's revenues and dispensed his justice within the shire. Jedburgh had a royal castle and was also given royal burghal status, although it lacked its own shire. Coldingham had its own shire, but was neither royal land (after the early 12th century) nor a burgh.

The establishment of monasticism, feudalism and

royal burghs gave the Borders a peaceful security and prosperity, which lasted, with only occasional interruptions, until the royal family died out in 1290. King Edward I of England used the rival claims by the Balliol and Bruce families to extend his influence over Scotland, which led to three centuries of open warfare or uneasy truce. An early result was the "Auld Alliance" between Scotland and France that was to bring French armies to the Borders and involve Scottish soldiers in desperate battles on behalf of France.

The wars saw the destruction of the older medieval castles and the development of the tower house as the distinctive military status symbol of the region. The rise in importance of a middle class in the later 15th and 16th centuries saw an increase in such places, and in the development of the bastle as the fortified home of the yeoman farmer or "bonnet *laird*".

By the end of the 14th century the number of monasteries had increased through the popularity of urban preaching friars, but abbeys and friaries suffered equally from the repeated assaults of English armies. The abbeys of Jedburgh and Kelso and the priory of Coldingham were actually turned into forts in the 1540s and had not fully recovered by 1560 when the Reformation in Scotland brought their lives to a close.

The Anglo-Scottish wars drew to a close with the Union of the Crowns in 1603, after which King James VI (I of England) suppressed the lawlessness that had characterised the frontier for centuries. The Border *Reivers* had made a living out of cattle rustling, burglary, kidnapping, blackmail and murder in the secure knowledge that the law would present no serious threat as long as there was enmity between Scotland and England. Their depredations are now part of Borders folklore and one explanation why the region has so many stone towers.

The long struggle with England was replaced by disagreement among Scots over what sort of religion Scotland would have and how it would relate to the government of the country. The king's determination to be head of the church, as in England, and opposition from radical *Covenanters* led to a series of wars in the 1630s and 1640s and

involved Scotland in a wider civil conflict.

The civil strife of the mid-17th century resulted in a short-lived republic under Oliver Cromwell, who succeeded where English kings had failed and established forts throughout Scotland. The restoration of monarchy in 1660 led to further religious persecution during the "Killing Times" but by the early 18th century Presbyterianism was established and other Protestant denominations tolerated. The net result of these divisions and others that were to occur later was the loss of all but a handful of the region's medieval churches and the deterioration and demolition of many of the new churches that had replaced them.

Enduring peace between Scotland and England led to the Act of Union in 1707 and created conditions under which a land-based economy could develop. This started in the countryside, where land reclamation and reorganisation, coupled with new farming techniques and better roads brought about an Agricultural Revolution. This developing prosperity was unaffected by the passage of Jacobite armies through the Borders in 1715 and 1745. On the other hand, wider access to education in Scotland assisted Borderers to positions of wealth and influence in the trading posts and colonies of the developing British Empire.

The new "castles" of the 18th and 19th century were large country houses set amid landscaped parks with walled gardens and home farms. New plantations and thousands of kilometres of hedges transformed the virtually treeless landscape of much of the Borders, where semi-natural woodland cover had reached its lowest level for several millennia. In the uplands sheep replaced arable farming and as a result many rural settlements shrank or disappeared entirely.

Increased food production improved the health of the population and sustained its growth. Such progress was at the expense of smallholders, who sought employment in those towns that were experiencing their own revolution in manufacturing through increased investment and technological innovation. Water powered mills enabled the Borders to establish a reputation for the production of textiles and the name of "tweed" was coined in the region.

Characteristic of the period is the huge range of original thought which took practical form in, for example, the new plough of James Small, the Union Bridge of Capt. Sir Samuel Brown, the writings of Sir Walter Scott and the many amenity and special interest societies which flourished from the 1840s and 50s. The exchange of ideas that provoked such outpourings was partly driven by developments in communication. Macadamised roads in the 18th century and steam driven railways from the 1840s greatly improved the transport network and were used to export textiles and bring in coal and lime, as well as people looking for work. Whereas these physically carried people and goods, newspapers, the "penny post", development of photography and the invention of the electric telegraph carried information and ideas.

Queen Victoria's Diamond Jubilee in 1897 marked the symbolic climax of the *Victorian* era. The rate of technological development continued to accelerate, even though the Borders, like Britain as a whole, had passed the peak of its industrial output. Borderers had spread over the globe, taking such surnames as Scott, Armstrong, Kerr (or Ker) and Chisholm to all parts of the English-speaking world. As a new century approached Borders communities celebrated by recalling the past. Market crosses, taken down a century earlier as a mark of progress, were re-erected and ancient ceremonies were revived, or invented.

The 20th century brought the greatest changes yet, from the first aeroplanes to space travel. It also saw the most terrible wars and the price paid is set out on memorials in every Borders community, while derelict airfields and air-raid shelters bear witness to the total nature of modern warfare. Empty factories, former railway lines and redundant churches are equally poignant monuments to former glories that have now joined medieval towers and prehistoric hill forts as part of the archaeology of the Borders.

The sites included in this book are places where close contact can be made with the history of the Borders. More can be learned about particular aspects of the past, from distant prehistory to events within living memory, in the other books in this series: Early Settlers in the Borders, Christian Heritage in the Borders, Warfare and Fortifications in the Borders and Farm and Factory: Revolution in the Borders and in the related website,
www.scottishbordersheritage.co.uk

Gazetteer of Heritage Sites

Gazetteer of Heritage Sites

Sites are located by number on the map on pages 78-79

1. Abbotsford House, Nr Galashiels; NT 508 342

Sir Walter Scott, pioneer of the historical novel, purchased a farmhouse with *"the unharmonious designation of Clarty Hole"* on the banks of the Tweed in 1812. Together with his family and servants, he moved into the farm which he renamed Abbotsford. Scott had plans for enlarging the house which were not carried out until 1818, and in 1822 the old house was entirely demolished, to be replaced by the main block of Abbotsford as it is today. Scott was a passionate collector of historic relics, including an impressive collection of armour and weapons, *Rob Roy's* gun and *Montrose's* sword, and over 9,000 rare volumes in his library. Visitors are able to see his study, library, drawing room, entrance hall and armouries, and the dining room overlooking the Tweed where he died on 21st September 1832. There are also extensive gardens and grounds and a private chapel, which was added after Scott's death. Open Seasonally. Admission Charge.

2. Ancrum Old Bridge; NT 638 237

Site of a skirmish in May 1549 in which English soldiers under the Earl of Rutland drove back a French force under General D'Essé, who had been charged with defending Jedburgh, but who had been forced to retreat to Ancrum. This bridge (**fig.1**) was built in c.1782 as part of the Carfraemill to Carter Bar *Turnpike*, which is now represented by the A68 Trunk Road. The bridge was due for demolition following the opening of the new bridge in 1938 but was retained as a wartime precaution, and embrasures for riflemen are built into the parapets. The bridge was restored in 1995.

Fig. 1 Ancrum Old Bridge was built as part of the Turnpike System around 1782. An earlier bridge on this site was the scene of a skirmish between English and French soldiers in 1549.

3. Ancrum Moor; NT 618 271

On 27 February 1545 this was the scene of a Scottish victory under the Earl of Angus over an English force under Sir Ralph Eure and Sir Brian Layton, who were retreating towards Jedburgh after a raid on Melrose. The course of the battle shifted decisively when the Teviotdale riders allied to the English changed sides.

The battlefield can best be appreciated from the path along Dere Street Roman road (no.36) where this crosses the ridge of Lilliardsedge. Beside the path at this point is an inscription to the heroic, but mythical maid Lillyard:

> *"Fair Maiden Lillyard lies under this stane;*
>
> *Little was her stature, but great was her fame;*
>
> *Upon the English loons she laid many thumps,*
>
> *and when her legs were smitten off, she fought upon her stumps".*

4. Ancrum Old Parish Church; NT 621 248

Virtually no trace survives of the earliest church at Alnecrumba, recorded in 1116 when the manor formed part of the diocese of Glasgow. The present structure was built in the 18th century and repaired in 1832, but after the construction of a new church within the village, fell into disuse and is now ruinous.

In the graveyard to the south of the ruins is a hogback, a Scandinavian-influenced grave marker, which takes its shape from a stylised long house and may pre-date the recorded 12th century church. Set on edge into one of the ruined windows is a carved stone with low relief decoration in the *Norman* style on two faces. This is likely to have come from the 12th century church and appears to represent two fantastic beasts.

5. Ancrum, Village Green & Market Cross; NT 628 245

The village still retains its central green with the market cross (front cover) that was set up as a focus for the regular markets that took place here from 1490. The patron who established this was Bishop Robert Blackadder of Glasgow, the feudal lord of the village. Like many small settlements in Scotland, this effort to develop the village as a commercial centre did not stand the test of time.

6. Ayton Old Parish Church; NT 927 609

The lands of *Eitun* were granted to the priory of Coldingham by King Edgar between 1098 and 1107 and before the close of the 12th century the monks erected a chapel here dedicated to St Dionysius (St Denis, also patron saint of France). This was used as a meeting place by Scottish and English Commissioners to negotiate treaties between the two kingdoms in 1380, 1384 and 1497. The chapel became the parish church after the Reformation, perhaps in 1627.

The old parish church appears to have been extensively altered and rebuilt in the 17th and 18th centuries when many of the original Norman features were removed or altered. Several burial vaults were subsequently built adjacent to the walls of the original church, including one for Alexander Skene (died 1823), commander of HMS Britannia. The present parish church stands close by and was erected in 1865.

7. Barns, Tower House; NT 215 391

The lands of Barns were acquired by the Burnet family during the 15th century and the small tower which they built stands on a slight mound beside the farm steading in the grounds of the 18th century Barns House. A window lintel bears the carved initials *WB MS* which suggest that the tower was built for William Burnet, the fourth laird of Barns, and Margaret Stewart of Shillinglaw, who were married in 1576. **Please note there is no public access to the tower, but it may be viewed from the road.**

8. *Bemersyde, Standing Stone; NT 594 338*

Early farming communities erected standing stones in the *Neolithic* and *Early Bronze Age* (6,000 to 3,500 years ago). The landscape at that time would have been very different, with vast forests of oak, elm and hazel inhabited by animals such as beaver, wolf, bear and *aurochs* (large wild cattle). Standing stones are generally considered to be religious or ceremonial monuments and this is one of several in this part of the Borders. The stone may have played a significant role in the landscape, perhaps marking the point where the Tweed emerges from the confines of Tweeddale into the flat country of the Merse. **Please note there is no public access to this monument, but it may be viewed from the road.**

9. *Birgham, Site Of Medieval Bridge; NT 789 390*

There has been a settlement at Birgham since the 7th century when the lower Tweed valley was part of the kingdom of *Bernicia*. The name Birgham derives from the Anglo-Saxon words "Brycg hâm" meaning "Bridge Settlement" and a bridge survived here until the *Middle Ages*.

The strategic importance of Birgham as a crossing point is highlighted by some important incidents in the history of Scotland and England. In 1018, King Malcolm II fought a decisive battle against Earl Uchtred of Northumbria at Carham, situated on the south bank of the river. This effectively set the lower Tweed as the Border with England. Of equal importance was the Treaty of Birgham, drawn up in 1290 after the death of King Alexander III. This treaty was an attempt by the Scottish nobles of the day to keep Scotland *"separate and divided, and free in itself, from the realm of England"* during marriage negotiations between the Scots and King Edward I.

10. *Blackhouse Tower, Nr Dryhope, St Mary's Loch; NT 280 272*

The Stewarts of Traquair who owned Blackhouse at the turn of the 16th and 17th centuries built this tower beside the Douglas Burn. The tower was one of many built in the Borders at a time when it was necessary to defend family and possessions from predatory attacks by neighbouring Scots and English raiders alike. **Blackhouse Tower is visible (but not accessible) from the Southern Upland Way.**

11. *Bowden Parish Church; NT 554 301*

The monks of Kelso Abbey founded the church of Bowden in about 1128. Very little of this ancient building still remains, save for some fragments in the west gable and north wall. The original church was a rectangular structure, to which *transepts* were added in the 15th century. The building has been remodelled at least twice since and still contains a rare survival in the "laird's loft" or family pew belonging to the Kerrs of Roxburghe.

12. *Bowhill, Nr Selkirk; NT 425 277*

Set within extensive policies (parkland) Bowhill is an impressive country house of the early 19th century with work by William Atkinson and William Burn for the Scotts of Buccleuch (**Plate 11**). The designed landscape around the house was laid out in 1832 by Thomas Gilpin, who created lochs, planted trees and used Newark Castle (**no.115**) as a feature ruin in the landscape. Today, Bowhill is the seat of the Duke of Buccleuch and, from 2003 will be home to the

James Hogg exhibition (currently at Aikwood Tower). Open Seasonally. Admission Charge.

13. Broughton, Dreva Craig; NT 126 353

On a prominent knoll 1.5km (1 mile) east of Broughton are a series of well preserved remains which represent changing land use in the Iron Age. A strong *hillfort* was constructed around the knoll in about the middle of the 1st millennium BC. This was enclosed by stone ramparts and reinforced to north and south by rows of earth-fast boulders, intended to break up or slow down any attacking formations. Some time later the hillfort was abandoned and a settlement comprising stone courts with circular houses inside was constructed over the northern stone rows and on the western slope below the hillfort.

Similarities between the farming practices of the Iron Age and those of today are reflected in the head-dyke which separated cultivated fields in the valley from the grazing of the hill and which can still be traced just upslope from its modern equivalent.

14. Broughton, Old Parish Church; NT 110 368

Upper Tweeddale once formed part of the Kingdom of *Strathclyde* and some medieval chapels in the area were dedicated to early Christian saints from the west. Kilbucho *(cille begha)* was "the chapel of St Begha", while at Broughton another was dedicated to St Llolan, a 7th century bishop. The existing remains probably date from 1726, when the church was extensively rebuilt. It was abandoned in 1803 when a new church was constructed at Calzeat (a short distance to the south) to serve the united parish of Broughton, Glenholm and Kilbucho and the older structure fell into decay.

Today, all that remains is the east gable and some

Fig. 2 Bunkle Old Parish Church is one of a small number in Scotland that still retain substantial 12th century Norman masonry. In this case a vaulted apse with slab roof is the sole survivor of the medieval church.

portions of the north and south walls. Against the south-east angle are the remains of a barrel-vaulted structure, perhaps a post-Reformation burial aisle. This was rebuilt in 1926-7 as a chapel in the belief that it represented the cell of St. Llolan.

15. Bunkle Old Parish Church; NT 808 596

A part of the original 12th century parish church of Bunkle still stand to their full height beside to the present church. Only the *chancel apse* remains (**fig.2**), but the narrow single-light windows, vaulted ceiling and flagged roof would have been typical of the many parish churches which were constructed in the Borders during the Norman religious revival. Bunkle was part of the *Bishopric* of Dunkeld and the present parish church (built 1820) contains some carved stones from the early period.

16. Capon Tree, Nr. Jedburgh; NT 650 188

In the 16th century much of the Jed Water valley still contained significant areas of woodland as part of the Royal hunting reserve of Jed Forest. Today a few ancient oak trees still survive, of which the Capon Tree is the best known and stands between the A68 trunk road and the Jed Water a little under 2km (1 mile) south of the town.

17. Cardrona Forest; NT 292 384

Cardrona Forest is situated on the south side of the River Tweed approximately 5km (3 miles) east of Peebles. There are parking and picnic facilities and three waymarked walks, two of which afford opportunities to view the remains of an Iron Age fort and Cardrona Tower (**fig.3**), a 16th century stronghold of the Govan family. Entrance to the tower was by a door in a corner stair turret. **Please note that there is no pubic access to the tower which may be viewed from the outside only.**

18. Carlops, Weaver's Village; NT 160 560

The existing village of Carlops was founded in 1784 when Robert Brown, laird of Newhall, began to establish a cotton-weaving industry. He laid out rows of weaver's cottages on each side of the main Edinburgh to Biggar road, immediately to the south of Carlops Bridge. In 1800 a West Linton weaver, Alexander Alexander, set up a water-powered woollen mill in the village, using coarse Tweeddale wool. This prosperity was short-lived, however, for the village failed to take advantage of the introduction of steam power and this led to a rapid decline in its importance. By the end of the 19th century it was little more than a summer health-resort, enjoying some renown on account of its associations with the poet Allan Ramsay.

19. Cessford Castle, Eckford; NT 738 238

This massive L-shaped tower overlooks the Kale Water and was built by the Kers of Cessford in the 14th century. A stone and earth rampart with an external ditch enclosed the tower. The castle was the subject of a dramatic siege in 1523 when an English force was foiled in an attempt to mine the central tower, although the owner later surrendered the place. **Please note that there is no public access to the castle, but it may be viewed from the adjacent track.**

20. Channelkirk Parish Church; NT 482 546.

There has been a church here from at least as early as the 12th century although the discovery of an early Christian long *cist* burial in the churchyard may indicate the presence of a much earlier church on or near this site. The present building was erected in 1817 and is one of the finest *Gothic Revival* churches in the Borders. It was designed by the master of the genre, James Gillespie Graham and still retains its original furnishings.

21. Chirnside Parish Church; NT 869 560

There was a parish church at Chirnside in the 12th century, when the *"ecclesia de Chirnyside"* was valued at 50 *merks*. Parts of the early building still survive in the present church. There is a Norman doorway on the south side of the church, but substantial remains of the early tower have been incorporated into the west end.

In 1524 the tower was used as a lookout point against English raiders. A group of six English reivers set upon the tower, which was stoutly defended by a young man named Luke Acheson. Acheson bravely fought against these raiders and they appeared to withdraw. Unfortunately for Acheson they had merely hidden nearby by and,

Fig. 3 *Cardrona Tower belonged to the Govan family and was one of sixteen towers in a 22km (14 mile) long stretch of the Tweed valley. Its vault now provides a temporary roost for bats.*

when he left the tower to raise the alarm in the village, they emerged and murdered him.

22. Cockburnspath Market Cross; NT 774 711

According to tradition the Market (or Mercat) Cross was erected in 1503 to commemorate the marriage of King James IV of Scotland to Margaret Tudor, sister of King Henry VIII of England (**fig.4**). The union of the two countries is symbolised by the thistle and the rose carved on the cross. A more likely, but less romantic interpretation, is that the cross dates to 1612, when James VI issued a charter to elevate the village to *Burgh of Barony* status. The combined flowers would represent the Union of the Crowns, which had followed the death of Queen Elizabeth I of England in 1603. The Cross marks the eastern terminus of the Southern Upland Way.

23. Cockburnspath Parish Church; NT 774 710

The parish of Cockburnspath was created in 1610 and the building can only have served as the parish church from that time (**Plate 13**). Formerly Cockburnspath stood within the parish of Old Hamstocks, now Oldhamstocks in East Lothian. Medieval records refer to a chapel, the property of Coldingham Priory, and a medieval hospital at Cockburnspath.

The church was occupied for a time by Oliver Cromwell's troops after the battle of Dunbar in 1650. The building was severely damaged by the encamped soldiers and not only needed repairs but also required a new roof.

24. Coldingham Priory; NT 903 659

Edgar, King of Scots gave land for a church at Coldingham and was present at its consecration in 1100; remains of this first building are exposed to the west of the present parish church. By the

Fig. 4 Cockburnspath Cross is carved with a thistle and a rose, but whether this was to symbolise a Royal marriage in 1503 or the Union of the Crowns a century later, is now disputed.

mid-12th century *Benedictine* monks from Durham had established a priory here, which was rebuilt by Prior Thomas of Melsonby after an attack by the English in 1216. The priory's wealth was based on income from a large estate and in the 13th century wool was exported as far as Italy, where merchants knew the priory as *Guldingamo*. However, its position close to the border and the wealth derived from trade and it's many estates meant that the priory became embroiled in fighting on more than one occasion.

In 1544 an Irish force (allied to the English) held the priory against a larger Scottish force and five years later Spanish troops (allied to the English) were taken by surprise by a body of French and

German troops (allied to the Scots) and either captured or slain. After the Reformation in 1560 the priory was not allowed to recruit new members and the parish took over the church. In 1648 Oliver Cromwell besieged the place and his artillery caused a gunpowder store within the church to explode, blowing out the south and west walls.

The present parish church incorporates the north and east walls of the monk's choir as rebuilt after 1216, while the churchyard contains remains of the south transept, cloister, chapter house and the refectory cellar, now known as "Edgar's Walls" (**fig.5**).

25. Coldstream, Coldstream Museum, Market Square; NT 843 397

This local history museum includes exhibits on the history of the town, the lifestyles of inhabitants in the area in the 18th and 19th centuries and the origin of the Coldstream Guards. Free Admission.

26. Coldstream, Henderson Park; NT 844 398

This centrally located park provides sweeping views across the River Tweed towards Northumberland and the Cheviot Hills. A monument located within the park records the town's association with the Coldstream Guards.

27. Coldstream, The Hirsel; NT 827 401

Situated 3.5km (2 miles) north-west of Coldstream, this estate has been the seat of the Earls of Home since the early 17th century. Excavations on the estate uncovered the foundations of an early Christian church, and are the subject of a permanent exhibition in the steading museum. The estate is open daily and also includes an exhibit on rural life on the estate,

Coldstream

Origins: In 1165 Cospatric, 3rd Earl of Dunbar founded a house of Cistercian monks and nuns at Coldstream with lands in the parishes of Lennel and Hirsel. A settlement developed outside the priory, which closed at the Reformation, and outgrew the older parochial centre at Lennel. Coldstream became a separate parish, incorporating the by now extinct parish of Hirsel, in 1718. Its importance as an entry point into Scotland was confirmed by the construction of James Smeaton's bridge in 1763-66.

Notable Events: 1165: Foundation of Coldstream Priory.

1545: Coldstream among numerous towns "brent, rased and caste down" by the Earl of Hertford.

1660: General Monck marched his regiment, now the Coldstream Guards, from here to support the Restoration of King Charles II.

Points of Interest: Civic Week (1st full week in August), Coldstream Museum (**25**), Henderson Park (**26**), The Hirsel (**27**), The Nun's Walk; the toll house for John Smeaton's bridge was the scene of runaway marriages until 1856, and is still known as 'the Marriage House'.

Fig. 5 *Coldingham Church still incorporates 13th century Gothic arcades and windows of the choir of the Benedictine Priory. Other remains of this ancient monastic house are visible in the churchyard.*

nature trails, the Hirsel Lake (a wildfowl sanctuary), and Dundock Wood, which is notable for its rhododendrons and azaleas. Open daily. Admission Charge.

28. Cove Harbour; NT 784 717

Cove Harbour occupies a tidal inlet among rocks, open to the east but enclosed on all other sides by high cliffs. The inlet has been a landing place since at least the beginning of the 17th century. In the 1750s and again in the 1820s attempts were made to build a harbour, but in each case the works were wrecked by storms before completion. The existing works, completed in 1831, consist of two piers that enclose a simple harbour and can be seen most clearly from the Southern Upland Way.

29. Craik Forest, Nr. Roberton; NT 345 079

Craik Forest is situated beside the upper Borthwick Water, approximately 16km (10 miles) south-west of Hawick. There are parking and picnic facilities, with extensive walks and cycle routes. Archaeological sites include the Roman road from Newstead to Carlisle, small Iron Age settlements, and a carved boulder known as the "Loupin' on Stane".

30. Cranshaws Parish Church; NT 692 618

Although the original church is said to have been dedicated to St. Ninian in the 7th century, the earliest documentary record of *"Craneshaues"* church dates from 1275. Sectarian strife in the 17th century saw the neglect of the church and a new church was built on the present site in 1739. The ruins of the old church still survive in the grounds of Cranshaws House. The new church was itself replaced by the present Cranshaws Kirk,

built in a neo-*Romanesque* style, in 1899.

Notable among the Victorian carvings of the church are a sundial (resting on the back of a grotesque personification of Time), *corbels* in the form of masks around the apse, and heraldic devices representing families who have owned the manor of Cranshaws in the past. The arms of the Royal House of Stuart are displayed inside the church on a tablet taken from the old church, where it was installed in King James VI's reign to remind the Reverend Alexander Swinton to offer prayers for the Royal Family.

31. Darnick; NT 531 343

Darnick was originally a grange (monastic farm) belonging to Melrose Abbey. It developed into a small community and by the 16th century it was protected by at least three tower houses. In common with many places in the Borders, Darnick suffered during the Anglo-Scottish wars and in September 1545 was recorded as having been *"brent, rased and caste down"* by an English force under the Earl of Hertford. Fisher's Tower was converted into a two-storey house in the 18th century, but is now ruinous and stands on the Main Street. Darnick Tower is still inhabited and stands close by. **Please note that there is no public access to either tower and that they may be viewed from the outside only.**

32. Dawston Burn, Battle of Degsastan; NY 567 980

The battle of Degsastan (AD603) would scarcely have compared with a skirmish in the Middle Ages. However, to Áedán mac Gabhráin, king of *Dalriada* and Aethelfrith, king of Bernicia, the fight was a decisive moment in their struggle for power in the Southern Uplands. Not much is known of the battle, but their war bands are believed to have met in the wild valley of the Dawston Burn at the head of Liddesdale **(Plate**

8), close to the point where the road from Kielder Water and North Tynedale enters Scotland.

Hering, son of Hussa (the previous king) led the Anglian force, which included King Aethelfrith's brother Theobald, a subordinate commander who perished with his followers. The Scotti fared worse, as almost the whole force was wiped out, and King Áedán's son Domingart was probably among those killed. The medieval Anglo-Saxon Chronicle records that *"never since has any Scottish king dared to lead an army into this nation"*.

33. Dawyck Botanical Garden; NT 167 351

Twenty-five hectares of landscaped gardens clothe the banks of Scrape Burn, a tributary of the River Tweed in the heart of the Tweedsmuir Hills. Dawyck is home to a fine collection historic conifers, many of which are outstanding examples of their kind. In addition to its wealth of North American species, Dawyck boasts famous plantings of unusual Asiatic Chinese trees, and is the source of the Dawyck Beech.

There is also a wide range of flowering shrubs, including the original Chinese collections of E.H. Wilson, which were sent from the Arnold Arboretum in America to the more favourable conditions at Dawyck. These include fine Rhododendrons, which provide the nucleus of an important collection of hardy species. There are carpets of flowering bulbs in spring, and a range of broad-leaved plants provides extravagant autumn colour, making Dawyck a delight for the visitor. Open Seasonally. Admission Charge.

34. Deepsykehead Kilns, Carlops; NT 169 546

In the 19th century this pair of double draw kilns processed local limestone for use in farming and construction. Rock was extracted from an adjacent quarry (now filled in), loaded into the top of the kilns and reduced to powdered lime by burning. When the powder had cooled, it was raked from the kiln and used on arable fields to reduce the acidity of the soil, or in mortar for building. **Please note that there is no public access to this monument which may be viewed from the road only.**

35. Denholm Green, Leyden Monument; NT 568 184

Near the centre of the village green in Denholm is a monument to the poet and scholar, Dr John Leyden. Leyden was an extremely talented scholar and accomplished linguist who helped Sir Walter Scott collect material for his *"Minstrelsy of the Scottish Borders"*. Leyden went on to become an important servant of the British Empire. He travelled widely and, together with Stamford Raffles and Lord Minto, was instrumental in the founding of Singapore. The cottage, where he was born in 1775, stands on the north side of the green.

36. Dere Street, Towford to St Boswells; NT 761 133 to NT 603 290

This was originally the strategic Roman road that led from the legionary fortress of *Eburacum* (York) to the northern frontier outposts near Perth (**fig.6**). The road was later used by early Christian missionaries, who established churches close by (for example at Jedburgh and Old Melrose) and also by invading armies such as the 6th century *Gododdin*. The fortifications on Peniel Heugh (**no.131**) may date from this early post-Roman

Fig. 6 *The Roman road, Dere Street, as seen here from the air and under snow, scarcely deviated in its course between the Cheviot and Eildon Hills*

Fig. 7 *Dryburgh Abbey stands in tranquil parkland beside the River Tweed and still retains the solitude of a rural medieval monastery.*

period and owe their existence to the proximity of the road. In 1545 Dere Street was used by the armies that met on Ancrum Moor (**no.3**).

37. Dryburgh Abbey; NT 591 316

This abbey was founded by the *Premonstratensian* Order in about 1150 under the patronage of Hugh de Morville, Constable of Scotland and Lord of Lauderdale. The abbey church was built in the later 12th and earlier 13th centuries, but has been severely quarried and little survives today (**fig.7**). The best preserved buildings are in the east cloister range, and include a 16th century *Commendator's House* inserted into the canon's dormitory. Like all of the Border Abbeys, Dryburgh was devastated on various occasions by English forces including 1322, 1385, 1544 and 1545. The abbey is the burial place of Sir Walter Scott, and Field Marshal Haig. In the care of Historic Scotland. Admission Charge.

38. Dryburgh, Temple of the Muses; NT 588 321

David Steurt Erskine, founder of the Society of Antiquaries of Scotland, bought Dryburgh Abbey in 1786 and landscaped the estate to include monuments to Scotland's history and culture, among them Wallace's Statue (**no.167**). The Temple of the Muses is a gazebo surmounted by a bust of Borders poet James Thomson, author of *The Seasons* and the lyrics to *Rule Britannia*. The original central statue of Apollo, long since removed, has been replaced by a modern figurative sculpture.

39. Dryhope Tower, St Mary's Loch; NT 267 246

Dryhope Tower (**fig.8**) stands to the north of St Mary's Loch, a short distance from the Southern Upland Way. This is one of many tower houses

Duns

Origins: *In the 13th century Duns was a town with a parish church, hospital of St Mary Magdalene and adjacent castle and deer park. Its history as a market town dates from 1489-90 and from 1903 until 1975 Duns served as the county town of Berwickshire.*

Name Derivation: *Most likely from the Anglo-Saxon word* dûn: *"a low hill with a flat summit".*

Notable Events: *June 1315: King Robert Bruce camps in the Park of Duns.*

July 1333: Scots muster at Duns before the Battle of Halidon Hill.

1377: Townsfolk repel an English invasion using cunningly fashioned devices.

1490: Duns erected a Burgh of Barony by King James IV in favour of George Home.

1545: Duns town one of many "brent, rased and caste down" by the Earl of Hertford.

1639: Covenanting army camps on Duns Law and raises the standard of the National Covenant

1650: Town garrisoned by Cromwell's troops.

1715: "Old Pretender" proclaimed at the Mercat Cross.

Notable Personages: *John Duns Scotus (c.1265-c.1308)*

Points of Interest: *Duns Law (40), Jim Clark Room (41), Reivers Week (1st full week in July), Town Trail.*

that were built in the Borders during the 15th and 16th centuries. It was home to Mary Scott, remembered in literature as the *"The Flower of Yarrow"* who was to marry the infamous Border reiver Walter Scott or "Auld Wat" of Harden. In 1592, King James VI ordered the tower to be demolished due to the participation of Scott on a raid, lead by Francis Stewart, Earl of Bothwell, against the king in his own palace at Falkland (Fife). Although now ruined and abandoned the tower still stands and while it is not accessible to the visitor it is an impressive monument to the troubled past of the Borders area.

40. Duns, Duns Law; NT 785 547

A path from Castle Street leads through the grounds of Duns Castle to the hill known as Duns Law. The summit is crowned by the low defensive banks of an Iron Age settlement, which may have given rise to a tradition that the original town of Duns stood on the hill. During the first Bishops' War of 1638 a Scottish army under General Leslie occupied the site. They left behind an unfinished fortification known as the "Covenanters' Redoubt". This was intended to be a substantial square earthwork enclosure with flanking bastions at each corner. The basic shape was laid out, but work ceased when the ramparts had scarcely reached knee height. Inside the enclosure is a recumbent boulder known as the "Covenanters' Stone" on which the standard of the National Covenant was reputedly raised.

41. Duns, Jim Clark Room; NT 782 538

This small museum is devoted to the career of Jim Clark, World Motor Racing Champion and Berwickshire Farmer. It houses a fascinating display of trophies, awards, photographs, model cars, memorabilia and video presentation. Open Seasonally. Admission Charge.

Fig. 8 *Dryhope Tower, a stronghold of the Scott family, stands beside the Southern Upland Way, close by St Mary's Loch.*

42. *Earlston Village; NT 575 384*

The village of Earlston is first mentioned as *"Ercheldun"* in the foundation charter of Melrose Abbey, which was granted by King David I in 1136. The town is renowned for a 13th century inhabitant, Thomas Rimour de Ercildoun, more commonly known as Thomas the Rhymer, who is said to have predicted the death of King Alexander III and to have been a guest of the Queen of the Fairies for seven years. Although a mutilated ruin on the south side of Earlston is known as Rhymer's Tower, it was not built until almost three hundred years after his death. **Please note there is no public access to Rhymer's Tower.**

43. *Eccles, Crosshall Cross; NT 760 422*

Half a mile north of the Eccles beside a minor road stands Crosshall Cross, a medieval stone cross that informed travellers that they had reached the boundaries of the *Cistercian* nunnery. The cross stands over 4m (13ft) tall and has carvings on all four sides. These include a man and greyhound beneath a cross (east), a stepped latin cross (north) a shield and sword beneath a cross (west) and a shield and sword (south). **Please note there is no public access to the cross which can be easily viewed from the roadside.**

44. *Eccles Parish Church and Cistercian Nunnery; NT 763 413*

The name Eccles is derived from the Latin word *ecclesia* (church) and is evidence of an early Christian presence here. Such an early church may have stood until shortly after 1250, when the church of St Andrew was extensively rebuilt. This was, in turn, replaced by the present building, which stands to the west of the original site, in 1774.

Gospatrick, Earl of Dunbar founded the Convent Church of St Mary the Virgin as a house of Cistercian nuns between 1145 and 1156. During the Anglo-Scottish Wars the house received the protection of a number of English kings and in 1523 the nuns spied for King Henry VIII during the siege of Wark Castle. In a reversal of fortunes, the priory met with disaster at the hands of the English during the 1540s, when the convent was seriously damaged on three occasions. There is no record of repairs to the nunnery, although Marion Hamilton was still prioress in 1566, and the property was later granted to the Hume family of Cowdenknowes. Fragments of the priory survive in the western boundary walls of the churchyard, where a blocked round-headed doorway may once have led from the nuns' church to the dormitory and cloister.

45. *Edin's Hall Broch, Abbey St Bathans; NT 772 603*

The striking gorge cut by the Whiteadder Water contains some of the oldest surviving woodland in the Borders, and provides an attractive approach to Edin's Hall *via* the Elba footbridge 1.6km (1 mile) to the east. Alternatively, the site may be reached from the west from Abbey St Bathans *via* Toot! Corner.

The original Iron Age settlement at Edin's Hall consisted of a fort, which is now represented by an oval enclosure defended by double ramparts, external ditches and entrances on the south and east. Around the end of the 1st millennium BC, the fort was reorganised and a large stone *broch*, or tower was built, along with several stone-walled houses and buildings inside the old fort (**fig.9**). The broch is the largest in area in Scotland and still stands more than 1.5m (5ft) high in places. The 5-6m (16-20ft) thick stone walls still contain rooms and the remains of a stairway to a now vanished upper storey. This site developed from a minor hillfort into a prestigious settlement and may have owed its status to the presence of copper mines nearby. A leaflet describing a circular walk

Fig. 9 *Edin's Hall broch was the most substantial building this Iron Age settlement and still stands over 1.5m (5 ft) in height. Access to the site is via a path along the scenic valley of the Whiteadder Water.*

taking in the broch is available from local Tourist Information Centres.

46. *Edrom Parish Church; NT 837 558*

A decorated Romanesque doorway from the original 12th century church now forms the entrance to the burial vault of the Logans of Edrom. The vault stands immediately to the west of the present church, which also incorporates the Blackadder chapel, founded by Robert Blackadder, bishop of Glasgow in 1499. The Logan Aisle is in the care of Historic Scotland.

47. *Eildon Hills, Melrose; NT 555 328*

The Eildon Hills are formed from hardened lavas that pushed up through layers of Old Red Sandstone around 350 million years ago. The volcanic rocks are also coloured red and are well exposed in an old quarry on the saddle between Mid Hill and North Hill.

North Hill is occupied by the largest hillfort in Scotland, which originated in the 10th century BC and still contains visible remains of nearly 300 *hut circles*. Although the site is traditionally described as a settlement, it may have operated chiefly as a ceremonial and social focus for the scattered hill communities of the region. In the early Roman period soldiers from *Trimontium* **(no.121)** built a watch tower on the summit and the shallow circular ditch which enclosed it is readily visible. Red Grouse can sometimes be seen from the Eildon Walk and St Cuthbert's Way, both of which cross the hills.

48. *Ettleton, Milnholm Cross and Ettleton Churchyard; NY 476 861 and NY 472 863*

Milnholm Cross, set up in memory of a laird of Mangerton (possibly Alexander Armstrong) stands within a railing in a field about 1.6km (1

Fig. 10 Ettleton parish no longer exists, but its churchyard still serves Newcastleton and contains grave slabs from the medieval church.

mile) south of Newcastleton. The cross is 3m (10ft) tall, although a modern top has been added. On the shaft, just below the cross-head, are the initials MA and AA in relief; below these is an incised sword with a rounded pommel and a straight cross-piece.

1.6km (1 mile) uphill is Ettleton churchyard, which provides fine views of the Liddel Valley. The parish of Ettleton was absorbed into Castleton parish in 1604, but although nothing survives of the medieval parish church, an impressive collection of medieval grave slabs has been preserved and built into the wall of an enclosure **(fig.10)**. The slabs include several carvings of crosses in low relief, including one with the chalice and bible of a priest.

49. Ettrick and Buccleuch Parish Church; NT 259 145

The Forest of Selkirk, Ettrick and Traquair was not finally cleared until post-medieval times and the "Kirk o' the Forest" is usually identified with Selkirk parish church. That a *"New Kirk of Ettrick"* existed by the early 16th century is, however, indicated by a record that in about 1561 the *"Kirks of Wester and New of Ettrick"* had paid no teinds (tithes) since the time of Flodden (1513). A panel on the tower of the present building dates it to 1824, and the plan and internal arrangements are those of a typical post-Reformation "preaching kirk". The tombs of James Hogg "the Ettrick Shepherd" and Tibbie Shiel can be seen in the churchyard.

50. Eyemouth, Eyemouth Museum; NT 945 642

This is a local museum of which the central point of the exhibitions is a magnificent tapestry, which was sewn by local women to commemorate the Great East Coast Fishing Disaster of 1881, when 189 local fishermen were drowned. The museum also houses exhibitions on historic local crafts and in particular Berwickshire's fishing heritage. Admission Charge.

51. Eyemouth, Fort Point and Corn Fort; NT 941 649

The headland provided a natural site for successive English and French artillery forts in the 16th century (fig.11). To the north-west, on the next headland are the remains of an Iron Age fortified settlement, known as the Corn Fort.

The earlier of the two artillery forts is English and was built in 1547. Because of its position, Eyemouth fort provided a base from which the occupiers could dominate the countryside and defend a staging post on the route between Berwick upon Tweed and English forts that had

---

Eyemouth

Origins: The town developed from the 12th century as the port of Coldingham Priory. The capture of Berwick by England in 1482 led to the development of Eyemouth as a port, its fortification in the 1540s, its charter as a market town in 1597-98 and its establishment as a separate parish in 1618. Eyemouth's later importance as a fishing port was largely the result of improved harbour works and connection to the east coast rail route.

Derivation: Settlement at the Mouth of the Eye Water.

Notable Events:

1547-57: English and French troops build artillery forts on Fort Point.

1597-8: Chartered as a Burgh of Barony.

1618: Eyemouth elevated to parish status.

1881: Eyemouth fishing disaster.

Points of Interest: *Eyemouth Museum (**50**), Fort Point & Corn Fort (**51**), Gunsgreen House, Herring Queen Festival (July), Town Trail.*

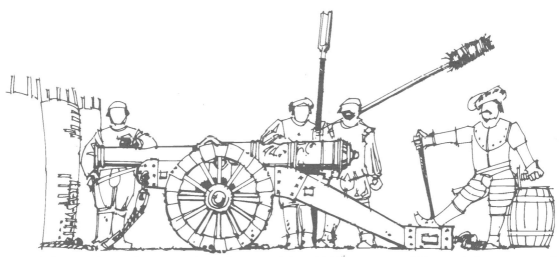

Fig. 11 *Cannon featured prominently in the wars of the mid-16th century and Eyemouth fort was one of several earthwork defences which were built in the Borders and designed, specifically, for the use of artillery. Drawing by David Pollack.*

been built in the Lothians. This fort was evacuated and demolished in 1550 and replaced by a larger, better-fortified French construction in 1557. Like it's predecessor, it also had a short lifespan and was demolished as part of a Treaty between England and France (and their various allies) in 1559. The ramparts of these fortifications still survive and the headland provides some spectacular views of rugged cliffs, which are the nesting place for many sea birds. The cliff path leads northwards to Coldingham and St Abbs Head.

52. *Ferniehirst Castle, Nr. Jedburgh; NT 652 179*

Ferniehirst was the seat of one of two main branches of the Ker family, and scene of actions in various wars, particularly when it was captured from the English by the French garrison of Jedburgh in 1549 **(fig.12)**. The lowest storey dates from the 16th century and was raised and extended from 1598. It is claimed that spiral staircases in the castle turn to allow the left-handed Kers to defend the upper floors from attackers. Paths lead

from the castle to the leafy Jed Water valley and other parts of the estate. Restricted summer opening times.

53. *Fogo Parish Church; NT 772 491*

There was a church at Fogo in 1159, when it was granted to Kelso Abbey, although nothing now remains of this first building. The present church is an architectural treasure and probably dates to a major rebuilding operation that took place in 1683. Although later additions and repairs have been made the church retains much of the character of the 17th century, with two laird's lofts, central pulpit and box pews.

54. *Foulden Teind Barn; NT 931 580*

Before the Reformation it is likely that a teind barn existed near every parish church. The teind barn at Foulden is one of only two such structures that survive in Scotland. These barns were used to store the teinds – that tenth part or tithe of a person's annual income or produce, which was

Fig. 12 *In 1549 Ferniehirst Castle, home of the Kers of Ferniehirst, was garrisoned by English soldiers until it was captured by a French force fighting on Scotland's behalf.*

owed to the church by ecclesiastical law. In the care of Historic Scotland.

55. Fulton Tower, Nr Bedrule; NT 605 158

Standing in a field beside the road from Bedrule to Easter Fodderlee, are the remains of Fulton Tower. Margaret Home of Cowdenknowes owned this 16th century tower house in the 1570s before her marriage to William Turnbull of Bedrule. Earlier in that same century the tower had been *"brent, rased and caste down"* by the Earl of Hertford. Surrounding the tower are the turf-covered foundations of houses and outbuildings connected with the tower. **Please note that this tower is on private land and may be seen from the roadside only.**

56. Galashiels, Englishmen's Sike; NT 504 351

According to local tradition a body of English soldiers was surprised near here whilst foraging for wild plums. The soldiers were defeated by local men and their bodies dumped into a nearby ditch, which is still known as "Englishmen's Sike". A commemorative stone, known locally as the "Raid Stane" is located adjacent to the Heriot Watt University Campus.

57. Galashiels, Gala Aisle; NT 494 357

The burial vault of the Scotts of Gala stands in the old parish churchyard. It is a small rectangular building of mixed whin and freestone rubble with freestone dressings. It was built in 1636 by

Galashiels

Origins: The place name suggests that the original settlement was a summer encampment or shieling for herdsmen, but by the later middle ages a village had developed and this was given a market charter in 1599. In the late 18th century Galashiels expanded onto the flood plain of the Gala Water and rapidly developed into a prosperous textile town, with ten woollen mills by 1828.

Derivation: Anglo-Saxon and Scandinavian: "The Shelters by the Full Stream".

Notable Events:

1337: Galashiels men defeat an English detachment at Englishman's Sike.

1503: Ettrick Forest lands gifted to Margaret Tudor by King James IV at Galashiels.

1599: Created a burgh.

Notable Personages: Thomas Clapperton (1879-1962), Andrew John Herbertson (1865-1915), Anne Redpath (1895-1965)

Points of Interest: Braw Lads Gathering (End of June, sometimes 1st weekend in July), Englishmen's Syke (56), Gala Aisle (57), Market Cross (58), Old Gala House (59), Town Trail.

Captain Hugh Scott of Gala and would originally have abutted the parish church. The Aisle was repaired and enlarged in the 19th century. Located within the Aisle is a memorial to Mark Duncan, a former Parish Minister who was killed at the Battle of Dunbar in 1651. Amongst the gravestones in the burial ground is the family tomb of Mungo Park, the African Explorer.

58. Galashiels, Market Cross; NT 492 357

The present cross was restored in 1887 and incorporates a 17th century sundial with a wrought iron weather vane dated 1695. The original cross was erected here as the focus of the market of Galashiels when the Pringles of Gala elevated it to a Burgh of Barony in 1599. The tolbooth and the parish church were also located around the market place, which formed the heart of the old town. Before the development of Scott Crescent in the 19th century, the main gate of the Pringles' (and later Scotts') residence of Old Gala House (see below) was located immediately behind the cross.

59. Galashiels, Old Gala House; NT 491 358

Old Gala House was originally a tower house of the Pringles of Gala built in 1457. This tower was incorporated into a larger building in 1583 and further expanded in 1611. The house and lairdship of Galashiels was acquired by the Scott family in the 17th century and was their home until 1876 when the family moved into New Gala House (now demolished). The house was further extended and modified in the 18th and 19th centuries and now serves as the local museum and art gallery. Old Gala House is set within its own grounds and houses the archive for the Border Family History Association. Admission Free.

60. *Gavinton Planned Village;*
NT 768 521

Gavinton is an early example of development by an improving landlord. In 1760 David Gavin, laird of Langton Estate, laid out a new settlement where his tenants could develop their cottage industries (principally weaving). At the same time he provided himself with more space around his own house by demolishing the original village of Langton and creating a landscaped park. The new village was named *"Gavintown"* after him.

61. *Glentress, Forest Walks, Iron Age*
fort, house reconstruction and
Viewpoint; NT 285 399

Glentress Forest is managed by the Forestry Commission and has been developed for public access. Miles of forest trails and paths give access to all parts of this man-made woodland for walkers, cyclists and horse riders. Historic features are interpreted for the visitor, and include the site of Shieldgreen Tower and the ramparts of an Iron Age hillfort on Janet's Brae. From the hillfort there are spectacular views of Peebles and Tweeddale, and a short walk leads to a reconstruction of a timber round house of the Iron Age period (**fig.13**). The woodland itself has a history, and some stands of Douglas Fir were planted in the 1920s, when the forest was created in response to the national shortage of timber brought about by the First World War. Parking charge.

62. *Greenknowe Tower, Gordon;*
NT 639 428

James Seton of Touch built Greenknowe Tower on a natural mound surrounded by marshy ground. The lintel over the front door bears the date 1581 (**fig.14**). The building is a classic L-shaped tower house and consists of a main rectangular block with a shorter wing. The tower is a type that would

not be out of place in the northern part of Scotland and is unique within the Borders. Cunningly sited gun loops would have provided virtually all-round cover of the courtyard that once surrounded the tower. In the care of Historic Scotland.

63. *Greenlaw Parish Church;*
NT 712 462

Greenlaw possesses an outstanding example of a 17th century Scottish parish church. It was constructed in or around 1675 and occupies the site of the pre-Reformation church, which was granted to the monks of Kelso in or after 1147.

In 1482 Berwickshire lost its traditional County Town (Berwick upon Tweed remains part of England), and from 1596 to 1903 it was administered from Greenlaw. A tower was built in 1712 to serve as a gaol with five cells on top of each other and a courtroom built to the west of the tower was used until the new Town Hall was completed. The church was subsequently extended westward to join the prison tower. The heavily barred tower and pieces of the former market cross now adjoin the church, although they were not original features.

64. *Harestanes Countryside Visitor*
Centre; NT 641 244

Harestanes Countryside Visitor Centre is managed by Scottish Borders Council and provides a wide variety of facilities for walkers and other visitors.

Harestanes was originally a farm in its own right, but was rebuilt in the 19th century as the Home farm steading for Monteviot Estate. The buildings are typical of a farm of the period and formerly included a sawmill, which stood in front of the entrance to the present visitor centre. The mill was powered by water from a millpond located across the field to the north-east. The millpond has recently been restored, although the lade which linked it to the mill has been filled in. By 1898 a

Fig. 13 *This reconstruction of an Iron Age house stands in Glentress Forest close to the Iron Age fort of Janet's Brae. Such circular structures were the standard building form throughout Britain 2,000 years ago.*

Fig. 14 *James Seton built Greenknowe Tower in 1581 and marked the occasion with his and his wife's initials and coats of arms above the entrance, which is a traditional Scottish iron "yett".*

new sawmill had been built to the north-west of the steading and is still in use.

A series of paths include the Waterloo Monument on the summit of Peniel Heugh (**no.131**) and link to St Cuthberts Way (**no.142**) and Dere Street (**no.36**). Harestanes, one of the most popular visitor attractions in Scottish Borders, offers a wide range of events, exhibitions and activities for all the family. Open Seasonally. Admission Free.

65. *Harlaw Muir Siting Tower, West Linton; NT 180 546*

On the north-west side of the road over Harlaw Muir is a square stone tower that served as a surveying point during the construction of the water conduit from Talla reservoir to Edinburgh in 1905 (**fig.15**). The whole project took ten years to complete and more than thirty men were killed in building the dam, laying a temporary railway and digging tunnels for the water main. Other sighting points are represented by concrete pylons on Harlaw Muir and at prominent hills between West Linton and upper Tweeddale. A short distance to the west of the tower are the grass covered remains of a Neolithic burial monument known as a long cairn. **The tower is no longer safe to enter and the visitor should only view it from the outside.**

66. *Hawick, Drumlanrig's Tower; NT 502 144*

The Douglases of Drumlanrig built this tower in the 16th century to dominate the crossing of the Slitrig Water, but subsequently lost it to the Scotts of Buccleuch. It played a part in the Anglo-Scottish wars and was seized by Covenanters during the "Killing Times" of King Charles II's reign. At the end of the 17th century Anne, Duchess of Buccleuch extended the L-plan tower to form her town house, which in c.1773 became a coaching inn and a focus for political meetings.

Hawick

Origins: Hawick developed on a ridge between the Slitrig Water and the River Teviot. In the 12th century the Norman family of Lovel built their castle to overlook the town and the parish church of St. Mary that stood beside it. By the later 16th century the town had grown across the Slitrig and along the High Street. Hawick was a burgh of barony with its own council and market by 1507, although it suffered from English incursions later in the century. Manufacture of cloth began in 1787 and quickly developed into the town's principal industry.

Derivation: Anglo-Saxon: "Haga + wic = hedge farm".

Notable Events:

1570: Hawick unthatched and burnt to save it from English attack.

1679: Drumlanrig's Tower seized by Covenanters.

1849: Railway arrives in Hawick.

Notable Personages: James Wilson (1805-60), James Lee Paris (1831-1904), Isobel Baillie (1895-1983), Jimmie Guthrie (1897-1937)

*Points of Interest: Common Riding (1st Friday and Saturday after the 1st Monday in June), Drumlanrig's Tower (**66**), Hawick Motte (**68**), Hawick Museum and Scott Gallery (**69**), Hornshole Battle Site (**67**), Town Trail.*

Fig. 15 *The construction of Talla Water Main between 1895 and 1905 was a complex engineering project and one of the relics associated with it is this sighting tower on Harlaw Muir.*

Recently restored, it contains a series of display galleries interpreting the turbulent history of the Tower and its former owners. Admission charge. Local Residents free.

67. Hawick, Hornshole Battle Site; NT 533 167

Beside Hornshole Bridge stands a cross marking the site where local tradition tells that a group of young men from Hawick overcame a band of armed English marauders in 1514. At the yearly "Common Riding" in early June a replica of the captured flag is carried by the "Cornet" (the leader of the festivities) in commemoration of the event.

68. Hawick Motte; NT 499 140

This flat-topped grass-covered mound is a Norman *motte* and was originally encircled by a defensive ditch and surmounted by a timber tower. The adjacent park was the site of an enclosed courtyard or *bailey*, although no visible traces remain. The motte probably dates from the 12th century when the Anglo-Norman family of Lovel was granted land in Hawick by King David I.

69. Hawick, Hawick Museum and Scott Gallery; NT 493 145

The building originated as Langlands House but had a history of rebuilding and alteration before the present structure was built in 1859. Since 1910 it has been a museum of local history, archaeology, social history, fine art and natural science, with particular reference to Hawick district and Teviotdale. The Museum and Gallery are situated within the grounds of Wilton Park, which is 43 hectares (107 acres) in extent and comprises attractive landscaped parkland and gardens beside the River Teviot.

70. Hermitage Castle; NY 496 960

Sir Nicholas de Soules, Lord of Liddesdale, built the castle of "Ermitage" sometime in the 12th century. However, the earliest part of the existing castle can be attributed to the Dacres, a Cumberland family who owned the place from 1358 until after 1365, when possession passed to the Douglases who developed it into the structure which survives today.

The Douglases held Hermitage until 1492 when it passed to Patrick Hepburn, Earl of Liddesdale. In the early 16th century *gun-loops* were inserted and the castle was provided with artillery. It was here in 1566 that Queen Mary visited her lover, Francis, Earl of Bothwell, who was resting after being wounded in a Border fray. Her ride over the moors and back from Jedburgh and consequent illness caused much scandal at the time. Although Hermitage was granted to the Scotts of Buccleuch in 1594, its importance as a Border stronghold was greatly diminished after King James VI succeeded to the English Crown and pacified the area a decade later. The castle was ruined by the late 18th century but the Duke of Buccleuch repaired the outer shell in 1820. In the care of Historic Scotland. Open Seasonally. Admission Charge.

71. Hermitage Chapel; NY 493 959

A short distance to the west of Hermitage Castle stand the remains of a small chapel and graveyard enclosed within an earlier set of earthworks. The chapel dates to the 13th or 14th century and contains a medieval gravestone bearing a carved cross and small sword. The earthworks, now best seen as a series of banks to the west of the chapel, may be the remains of a type of defended farmstead that was common in Norman England during the 12th and 13th centuries.

Between the south wall of the graveyard and the riverbank lies the "Cout o' Kielder's Grave", a low mound with fragments of tombstones at each end. Traditionally this is the grave of Sir Richard Knout (Knut), of Kielder in Tynedale, Sheriff of Northumberland, who died around 1290.

72. *Hume Castle; NT 704 413*

The castle was the seat of the Hume or Home family from at least the 13th century until 1515 when the Regent Albany executed Alexander, 2nd Lord Home and his brother for treasonable dealings with England. Thereafter the castle was dismantled, but in 1519 Sir James Hamilton of Finnart spent £690 on rebuilding it. The Homes regained possession and the castle played an important part in the wars of the 1540s. It held out successfully against the Earl of Hertford's troops during the raid of 1545, but was surrendered by Lady Home two years later when her son (who had been captured at the Battle of Pinkie) was brought up before the walls and threatened with death. The castle was recovered in 1548 and garrisoned by French troops. A century later, Colonel Fenwick bombarded the castle with mortars and captured it on behalf of Oliver Cromwell (1650), after which it was demolished.

The castle is a rare example of a simple courtyard castle of the 13th century and the ruined curtain wall forms the base of a folly built in 1794 for the last Earl of Marchmont. A viewpoint at the southwest corner affords extensive views across the Merse to the Cheviot and Lammermuir Hills and the volcanic peaks of the central Borders. In the care of Berwickshire Civic Society.

73. *Hume Old Parish Church; NT 700 408*

The church was built before 1127 when Orm or Horm was the parish priest. The church was dedicated to St. Nicholas by Robert, bishop of St. Andrews in April 1147, and served the parish of Hume until it was merged with Stichill sometime

before 1620. The church is reported as having been destroyed by Cromwell's troops in 1653 and described as ruinous twenty years later (1673). Only the outline of the building now survives in the north-east corner of the graveyard.

74. *Hutton Parish Church; NT 907 540*

The earliest record of a parish church here is in 1243. Although a new church replaced the original in 1765, it was demolished due to poor repair in 1834. The present church dates from 1835 and is one of the earliest Romanesque revival churches in Scotland. The churchyard contains many interesting gravestones, several of which date from the 17th century.

75. *Innerleithen, Early Cross Shaft; NT 332 369*

The base of a stone shaft stands against the east wall of Innerleithen Parish Church (**fig.16**). It was formerly part of the foundations of the old Parish Church and is decorated with abstract designs. Although the nature of the decoration is more reminiscent of prehistoric art, the stone is believed to date to the 9th century AD and to have formed the lower part of a cross, which may have provided a focal point for early Christian preachers.

76. *Innerleithen, Pirn Hill; NT 335 372*

Situated on Pirn Hill overlooking the Leithen Water are the remains of a 2,000 year old hillfort. This settlement is enclosed by two defensive ramparts, with more visible on the north side. In the interior are traces of terraced areas where wooden roundhouses would have stood. On the summit of the hill is a ring of stone cairns built to represent the size and shape of one of these stone houses and on the cairns are pictorial carvings based on local historical themes. Excellent views

Innerleithen

Origins: *The medieval village of Innerleithen developed alongside the Leithen water and grew into a town only in the late 18th and 19th centuries, following the opening of Caerlee Mill, the first modern woollen manufactory of the Borders, in 1788. The spa of St. Ronan's Well attracted visitors in the early 19th century, particularly after the publication of Sir Walter Scott's novel of the same name in 1823.*

Derivation: *Old Irish:* "inver + leithen = mouth of the River Leithen"

Notable Events: *1788: Caerlee Mill opens.*

1823: "St Ronan's Well" published.

Notable Personages: *Alexander Brodie (18th century)*

Points of Interest: *Cleikum Festival (August), Early Cross Shaft (75), Pirn Hill (76), Robert Smail's Print Works (77), St. Ronan's Wells Visitor Centre (78).*

Fig. 16 *This carved stone was found during the demolition of the former parish church of Innerleithen and is thought to be part of an early Christian cross.*

of the Tweed valley may also be had from this elevated vantage point. Access to the site is signposted from Leithen Road and is linked to a network of forest paths.

77. Innerleithen, Roberts Smail's Print Works; NT 332 367

This printing works has been completely restored and contains an office, composing and press rooms and a paper store with reconstructed water-wheel. Visitors can discover the secrets of the printing works from archive-based posters, by watching the printer at work and by trying typesetting by hand. Many historic items and photographs on display also give a fascinating insight into this small Borders town. Open seasonally. Admission Charge.

78. Innerleithen, St Ronan's Wells Visitor Centre; NT 328 372

This Visitor Centre tells the story of St Ronan's Wells, immortalised by Sir Walter Scott in his novel of the same name. The visitor may also sample the "waters". Fine views over the village and across the Tweed valley may be gained from the site. Open Seasonally.

79. Jedburgh Abbey; NT 650 204

The 12th century abbey church is one of Scotland's most outstanding medieval buildings and was founded by King David I in 1138 **(Plate 10)**. This house of *Augustinian* canons from Beauvais in France was deliberately located close to the site of an earlier Anglo-Saxon monastery and stones from a nearby Roman fort can be seen in its fabric. King Alexander III was married to Yolande de Dreux here in 1285 and King Edward I of England stayed here during the Wars of Independence (his soldiers took the roofing lead for siege engines). The abbey (and the town) bore the brunt of attacks by the English and their allies seven times between 1409 and 1545 and was fortified in 1548 by French allies of the Scots. The story of the abbey is told in an interpretation centre and the cloister and domestic ranges have been excavated and laid out to view. In the care of Historic Scotland. Admission charge.

80. Jedburgh, Canongate Bridge; NT 650 203

Up to the 18th century the road from England crossed the Jed Water at this point and entered the town *via* the Canongate. In the 16th century the present bridge was constructed and carved stones taken from the windows and doors of the town's ruined *Franciscan* friary can be seen built into the parapets. The bridge incorporates the narrow arch of an older pack horse bridge.

81. Jedburgh, Castle Jail and Museum, Castlegate; NT 648 202

Originally, a Howard Reform prison dating from 1824, the building now incorporates a museum of local history and retains displays on prison life within the cell blocks **(fig.17)**. It stands on the site of the Royal Castle of Jedburgh, which was destroyed in 1409. Admission charge. Local Residents free.

Jedburgh

Origins: Jedburgh is the oldest documented Borders town. An Anglian monastery and settlement existed at "Geddewrda" in the 9th century and were succeeded in the 12th by a Norman abbey, Royal castle and burgh. Despite three centuries of warfare, this frontier town succeeded Roxburgh as the county town and continued in the role until 1975. The town became an important staging post for travellers on the turnpike between Newcastle and Edinburgh in the 18th century and developed as a woollen manufactory in the 19th century.

Deviation: Anglo-Saxon: "worth" – the settlement by the Jed Water.

Notable Events: c.1138: Foundation of Jedburgh Abbey.

12th century: Granted Royal Burgh Status.

The town and abbey suffered English attacks in 1409, 1410, 1416, 1464, 1523, 1544 and 1545.

c.1500: Foundation of Jedburgh Greyfriars.

1566: Queen Mary stayed in Jedburgh.

1745: Charles Edward Stuart ("Bonnie Prince Charlie") stopped in Jedburgh.

Notable Personages: John Ainslie (1745-1828), Mary Somerville (780-1872), Sir David Brewster (1781-1868)

Points of Interest: Abbey (79), Callants Festival (1st two weeks in July, ends 2nd Saturday in July), Canongate Bridge (80), Castle Jail and Museum (81), Greyfriars Garden (82), Mary, Queen of Scots Visitor Centre (83), Town Trail.

Fig. 17 *Jedburgh Castle Jail, now a museum, was built in 1824 on the site of the medieval royal castle. In this model prison the three separate cellblocks could be supervised from a central point in the main building.*

82. *Jedburgh, Greyfriars Garden;* NT 650 208

The foundations of the last monastic house to be founded in Scotland are visible in this garden. Many medicinal herbs and local varieties of fruit tree are to be seen here, and interpretation tells the story of the 16th century house of Franciscan friars and its destruction at the hands of English gunners in 1545.

83. *Jedburgh, Mary, Queen of Scots Visitor Centre;* NT 651 206

A 9th century Northumbrian cross base stands in the gardens and although badly damaged, carvings of fantastic beasts can still be traced. Such crosses played a part in the preaching activities of early Christian missionaries. The Visitor Centre is housed in a 16th century bastle house, to which a wing was added in the 17th century. Displays interpret the life and times of Mary, Queen of Scots, who according to local tradition, stayed in the house after having visited her lover, the Earl of Bothwell at Hermitage Castle (**no.70**) in 1566. Admission Charge. Local Residents free.

84. *Kelso Abbey;* NT 728 338

Tironensian monks moved here from Selkirk around 1128 and founded the oldest and, at one time, the largest of the Border Abbeys. Kelso was very wealthy and this, coupled with its proximity to the English Border, meant that the abbey was a natural target for marauding English armies. The buildings were attacked on several occasions before finally being dismantled by Spanish mercenaries on behalf of the Earl of Hertford in 1545. However, the impressive west end of the Romanesque church with its unusual transepts and central tower still survives. In the care of Historic Scotland.

85. *Kelso Bridge;* NT 727 336

The elegant five span bridge which crosses the River Tweed at the entrance to the medieval burgh of Kelso was designed by John Rennie and constructed between 1800-03. This bridge replaces an earlier one that had been swept away during a flood in 1797. At the eastern end of the bridge is a tollhouse of the same date and beyond this, a pillbox with gun-loops built by home defence forces during the Second World War.

86. *Kelso, Floors Castle;* NT 711 346

To the north of the town, within easy walking distance of the Town Square is Floors Castle (reputedly the largest house in Scotland). It was designed and built for the 1st Duke of Roxburghe by William Adam in 1721-26. Adam also laid out most of the surrounding designed landscape and took some of the building materials from Cessford Castle, near Eckford (**no.19**). The house was extensively remodelled in 1837-45 by William H Playfair to give it the imposing appearance that it has today. Floors is set within an extensive designed landscape, which may be explored by the visitor. The house is privately owned by the present Duke of Roxburghe but is open to the public. Admission Charge.

87. *Kelso, Junction Pool;* NT 725 338

The River Tweed enjoys world-wide fame among fishermen as a great salmon river and the Junction Pool, where the Tweed and Teviot meet, is its most celebrated beat. A viewpoint on the Right Bank tells the story of the pool and provides opportunities to watch fish leaping and anglers at work.

Plate 1. The valley occupied by Mire Loch separates the hard volcanic rocks of St Abbs Head from the sedimentary rocks that underlie most of the Borders and which were formed between 500 and 400 million years ago. The headland is noted for its seabirds, plant life and the site of an early Christian monastery.

Plate 2. The distinctive hill of Rubers Law is just one of many isolated hills in the central Borders that erupted as volcanoes around 350 million years ago. Its natural defensive qualities and all-round views attracted early settlers, as well as Covenanters who held open-air services or "conventicles" here during the religious persecution of the late 17th century.

Plate 3. Bedshiel Esker is a winding gravel ridge, which was deposited by a stream flowing beneath a melting ice sheet towards the end of the Ice Age. In the Borders, glaciers deepened valleys and rounded off hills and deposited clays, sands and gravels in lowland areas, where they have had a lasting influence on subsequent plant, animal and human activities.

Plate 4. The Whiteadder Water cuts a deep channel through the glacial clays and underlying sandstones of the Merse. A wide variety of wildlife habitats exist on the valley sides where woodland has not been cleared for cultivation.

Plate 5. Relics of prehistoric societies are prolific in the Borders. On the shores of West Water Reservoir in the Pentland Hills, archaeologists excavated a Bronze Age cemetery in 1992. The stone chambers that contained the burials have since been re-erected at West Linton.

Plate 6. Iron Age forts on crests, cultivation terraces on hillsides and undefended settlements on lower slopes are typical archaeological features of the Borders hills where, for thousands of years, farmers struggled to subsist in a challenging environment.

Plate 7. Soldiers of the Roman Army crossed the Cheviot Hills on their way to the northern frontier. The view from Dere Street towards the Cheviot (815m/ 2,674ft) may have given them a foretaste of what they would encounter further north.

Plate 8. In AD603 the Battle of Degsastan was fought in this remote valley where the Dawston Burn flows. The encounter helped to establish English-speaking peoples in the Tweed valley centuries before Scotland or England became political entities.

Plate 9. The picnic site in Thornylee Forest looks across the Tweed towards the medieval Elibank Castle, a stronghold of the Murray family in the dark days of the Border Reivers and home to legendary "Muckle-Mou'd" Meg. The story of Meg is told in words and sculpture at the picnic site.

Plate 10. Jedburgh Abbey is as old as the nation of Scotland herself, although the magnificent ruins date mainly from the 12th century. The abbey and the Royal Burgh bore the brunt of many attacks from English armies during the Middle Ages.

Plate 11. By the mid-18th century, when the Dukes of Buccleuch began to develop Bowhill, scant remains existed of the once extensive Ettrick Forest. Over the following hundred years marshes were drained, fields enclosed and hedged, trees planted and cottages rebuilt, transforming the rural landscape and way of life.

Plate 12. Kelso developed around the great medieval abbey, but by the 18th century had also become a prosperous market town with many fine houses. In 1803 a new bridge of revolutionary design opened across the River Tweed as part of the new nation-wide turnpike system that enabled much easier movement of people and goods around the country.

Plate 13. The curious church of Cockburnspath has survived, whereas many in the Borders no longer remain. Even where no church exists, however, the graveyard usually remains as a source of interest, particularly to those whose ancestors left the Borders to start a new life in a different part of the world.

Plate 14. The independent spirit of Borders towns is expressed in annual festivals. Selkirk Common Riding, seen here, incorporates one of the largest cavalcades of any European festival and has its origins in medieval times.

Plate 15. The visual arts are part of the Borders heritage and are not confined to galleries, museums or private collections. This sculpture at Tweed's Well depicts the river from source to sea and is the first of a series of viewpoints recently developed along the course of the Tweed.

Plate 16. Landscape and folklore have been an inspiration to Borders writers from at least the time of Thomas the Rhymer in the 13th century. The triple-peaked Eildon Hills were a particular favourite of Sir Walter Scott, whose horse paused at his favourite viewpoint, even when taking his master to be buried at Dryburgh.

Kelso

Origins: *Kelso Abbey was established across the river Tweed from the royal burgh of Roxburgh in 1128. The settlement that grew up outside the monastic precinct was an ecclesiastical burgh by 1237 under the patronage of one of Scotland's wealthiest abbeys. The decline of Roxburgh in the 15th and 16th centuries removed the town's closest trading rival, but Kelso suffered a number of setbacks through war, closure of the abbey and two accidental fires. In the 18th century the town prospered from the rich farmland of the Merse and became popular with Edinburgh society as a country retreat. Agriculture remains the chief source of Kelso's wealth.*

Notable Events:

1128: Foundation of Kelso Abbey.

1523: English soldiers burn town.

1545: Earl of Hertford's troops sack abbey.

1644: Great Fire of Kelso destroyed most of town.

1685: Second Fire of Kelso.

1715: Old Pretender proclaimed at Wester Kelso.

Notable Personages: *Sir William Fairbairn (1789-1874), Sir James Brunlees (1816-92).*

Points of Interest: *Abbey (84), Civic Week (middle of July), Floors Castle (86), Junction Pool (87), Kelso Bridge (85), Maxwellheugh Viewpoint (88), Parish Church (89).*

88. Kelso, Maxwellheugh Viewpoint; NT 728 333

This viewpoint was developed to celebrate the Millennium and provides a panorama of Kelso Bridge, town and abbey **(Plate 12)**. This part of the town was originally in the parish of Maxwell (*"Maccus' Well"* in the 12th century) and the home of the first people to bear that surname.

89. Kelso Parish Church; NT 729 339

This unusually shaped building was built in 1773 and recently restored. James Nisbet, who also designed nearby Ednam House, was the architect of this octagonal church. The adjoining graveyard had been the cemetery of Kelso Abbey before the Reformation of 1560.

90. Kilnsike, Bastle House, Nr Jedburgh; NT 634 130

This is a good example of a 16th century bastle, or fortified farmhouse. This structure, built of massive boulders held together with clay, provided shelter from raiders (reivers) in the days before the Union of the Crowns in 1603. A lower floor provided a store and protection for a few livestock, while a movable stair and a virtual absence of windows gave defenders the means to hold out on the upper floor until help could arrive. **Please note that the tower stands on private ground and may be viewed from the roadside only.**

91. Ladykirk Parish Church; NT 888 476

This parish church was built c.1500, reputedly on the orders of King James IV after he nearly drowned when attempting to ford the Tweed. The church was the scene of the signing of part of the Treaty of Cateau-Cambresis in 1559, which was the last peace treaty between England and

Scotland before the Union of the Crowns in 1603. This exceptionally sturdy cruciform church has a slab roof supported by vaulted ceilings throughout and is the most complete Pre-Reformation church still in use in the Borders.

92. *Lamberton Old Parish Church; NT 968 573*

Lamberton consisted of two townships of Over and Nether Lamberton, which were granted to the monks of St. Cuthbert at Durham in 1095 and later became a chapel of Coldingham Priory. The chapel was dedicated to St Lambert, Bishop of Maastrict in Holland, who died a martyr in AD709. Lamberton was absorbed into the parish of Mordington in 1650.

It was within this church that the Scottish Commissioners received Princess Margaret of England on her way to marry James IV in 1502. In 1573 the Treaty of Lamberton was signed in the church to allow an English army to besiege and take Edinburgh Castle from the supporters of Mary Stewart on behalf of her son, the young King James VI.

The present remains represent the burial vaults of the Rentons of Lamberton and the Logans of Lintlaw and Burnhouse.

Fig. 18 *Many Borders settlements contained several defensive towers, but most have long since gone. Langshaw still retains three: Hillslap (centre left), Colmslie (upper centre) and Langshaw Tower (centre right).*

93. Langshaw, Colmslie, Hillslap and Langshaw Towers; NT 513 396, NT 513 393 and NT 517 397.

Situated in a minor valley to the north of Galashiels is Langshaw, a rural settlement made remarkable by the presence of three 16th century stone towers (**fig.18**). Hillslap and Colmslie were built by members of the Cairncross family, while Langshaw was erected by the Pringles. Although King Malcolm IV granted the rights to build a cow shed at *"Cumbesley"* in the mid-12th century, there is no evidence for a tower here before the Cairncross stronghold.

Although it is now unusual to find three towers so close together, many medieval settlements had such groupings which have disappeared. There were twelve stone bastles at *Lessuden* (modern St Boswells), Jedburgh had six and nearby Darnick still has two. **Please note these towers can only be viewed from the road and that there is no public access.**

94. Lauder, Thirlestane Castle; NT 533 479

The probable site of the motte and bailey castle of the Norman Morville family was used to create a large artillery fort during the English occupation of 1548. This was dismantled shortly after, but the site was reoccupied in 1590 when the Maitland family built the present castle (**fig.19**) and named it after their ancestral tower on the east side of Lauderdale. The house was enlarged by William Bruce for the 1st Duke of Lauderdale in 1673 and incorporates some superb plaster ceilings by workmen who had previously decorated Holyrood Palace. Open Seasonally. Admission Charge.

Lauder

Origins: *The town developed beside the ancient Roman road, Dere Street in the 12th century and was dominated by the castle of the de Morvilles. Early burgh charters were destroyed during the Wars of Independence and the oldest surviving dates from 1502. In 1548 an artillery fort was constructed by the English on the site of the Morvilles' castle, but was dismantled two years later by peace agreement. In 1590 Thirlestane Castle was built on the site. The town developed into a coaching stop on the Edinburgh to Newcastle turnpike, but even now has barely outgrown its medieval boundaries and still retains its "Burgess Acres", which are a unique survival of the pre-enclosure open field system.*

Notable Events:

1482: Murder of some of the king's favourites by jealous nobles led by Archibald "Bell the Cat" Douglas, 5th Earl of Angus.

1502: James IV renewed rights of burgh of Lauder by charter.

1550: Siege of Lauder fort by Scottish forces.

Points of Interest: *Common Riding (1st Saturday in August), Thirlestane Castle (**94**), Town Trail.*

Fig. 19 This prominent site beside the Leader Water was occupied in turn by the medieval castle of the de Morvilles, an English artillery fort of 1548 and finally by Thirlestane Castle (built c.1590).

95. *Leaderfoot, Viaduct and Bridges; NT 575 345*

Three bridges cross the Tweed at Leaderfoot and these are best seen from the viewpoint at the south end of the oldest, central bridge. The first structure at this point, now long gone, would have carried the Roman road, Dere Street on its way from the nearby fort of Trimontium (**no.121**) to the northern frontier of the Empire on the edge of the Highlands.

Alexander Stevens built the old road bridge in 1779-80 to carry a new Turnpike between Jedburgh and Edinburgh. This bridge is now closed to motor vehicles and carries part of the Tweed Cycle Way. In 1865 the magnificent Leaderfoot Viaduct of thirteen arches was constructed for the St Boswells Junction to Reston section of the Berwickshire Railway, a line which closed in 1948. The most recent bridge carries the A68 trunk road and was built in 1971-73. **Please note there is no public access to the Leaderfoot Viaduct, which may be viewed from the roadside only.**

96. *Legerwood Farm Trail;*
NT 586 433

Situated in the midst of Lauderdale, Legerwood Farm lies midway between the sheep farms of the Southern Uplands (to the west) and the lower fertile arable farms of the Merse (to the east). It is a typical farm of this area, comprising mixed livestock and arable. The farm trail is open to the public and provides an opportunity to see a variety of breeds of plant and animal, as well as to enjoy the wildlife of the field margins and hedgerows.

97. *Legerwood Parish Church;*
NT 594 434

There has been a church on this site from at least as early as 1127, when John, priest of *"Ledgaresude"* bore witness to a charter. In 1164 Walter de Lauder granted the church to the monks of Paisley Abbey, who held it until the Reformation in 1650. *"Walter, Vicar of Lichardswode* (Legerwood)" was among the Scottish nobility who swore fealty to King Edward I of England after his capture of Berwick in 1296.

Despite later remodelling, the church retains its Norman chancel arch and other carved stones.

98. *Lempitlaw Churchyard;*
NT 786 326

In 1122 Richard Gernun (or Germyne) granted Lempitlaw Church to the House of the Holy Trinity of Soltre (Soutra). Originally a parish in its own right, Lempitlaw was unified with Sprouston after the Reformation. The parish church stood until the late 18th century but now survives only as grass covered foundations from which a two cell building of chancel and *nave* can be discerned. The chancel contains a fine hogback tombstone of Anglo-Scandinavian inspiration **(fig.20)**.

99. *Lennel Old Parish Church;*
NT 857 411

The church of *Leinhah* (Lennel) was in existence in the early 12th century and was the parish church for the village that formerly stood to the east. David de Bernham, Bishop of St. Andrews,

Fig. 20 *This hogback tombstone at Lempitlaw is a relic of 10th century Anglo-Scandinavian settlers who covered their graves with stones carved to resemble shingle-roofed houses.*

dedicated the church to St. Mary on 31 March 1243. During the 12th century the revenues from the lands of Lennel church were shared equally between the priories of Coldingham and Coldstream, but by the early 13th century rights to those belonged solely to the Convent of St. Mary at Coldstream. Two early 19th century graves in the churchyard are covered by iron *mort-safes* to insure against grave robbers, or "resurrectionists".

100. *Liddel Castle, Nr Newcastleton; NY 509 899*

On a bluff overlooking the Liddel Water are the remains of a 12th century earthwork castle built by Ranulph de Soules, one of the Norman settlers to whom King David I granted lands. On the opposite side of the road is the site of the former village of Castleton and beside the castle is St Martin's Churchyard. King David I granted the medieval church that stood here to the monks of Jedburgh Abbey. Nothing now remains of either the church or the village and it is hard to imagine that this was once the site of a thriving community. **Please note that Liddel Castle is not accessible to the public and should only be viewed from the road.**

101. *Lindean Reservoir, Nr Selkirk; NT 503 291*

Lindean Reservoir is a relatively new feature in the Borders landscape, having been created by South East of Scotland Water Board in 1904. The site has, however, a much longer history. The area was originally known as Wester Lang Moss, a marsh that formed after the last Ice Age. The moss was drained and excavated to provide marl (lime rich clay) during the Agricultural Revolution in the 18th and 19th centuries. The resulting hollow filled with water and formed the basis for the new reservoir.

No longer used for its water, Lindean is home to a variety of plant, animal, bird and insect species

including water plantain (spectacular in May when it flowers), Reed Bunting and Little Grebe. There is a path around the reservoir, disabled access to part of the site and on-site information. A leaflet with more information on the site is available from local Tourist Information Centres.

102. *Longnewton Old Parish Church; NT 577 273*

In the 18th century Longnewton village and its adjacent churchyard occupied land where now only a curious little country graveyard exists in isolation among farmland **(fig.21)**. The village was there in the 12th century and in 1220 the chapel of *Longa Neutun* became its parish church. In 1684 the parish was absorbed into that of Ancrum and the church became redundant, although burials continued to be made up to the 1870s. A depression in the turf indicates the site and small size of the church itself and there are several 18th century decorated gravestones in the churchyard.

103. *Lyne, Roman Fort; NT 188 405*

This is the best preserved Roman fort in the Borders and was built in the 2nd century AD. Its rampart and defensive ditches can be traced for much of their course around the perimeter of this playing-card shaped fort. Entrances on the east, south and west can still be identified, although ploughing has levelled the interior, where the garrison would have been quartered in barrack blocks arranged around a central headquarters building. Access to the fort is from the lane that leads to Lyne Parish Church.

104. *Lyne Parish Church; NT 191 405*

During the reign of King William the Lion (1165-1214) the chapel of Lyne was owned by the Bishops of Glasgow and was a dependant of Stobo Church. It became a parish church in it's own

Fig. 21 Many Borders' graveyards no longer contain a church, but were used for burial until relatively recently. Longnewton churchyard is particularly isolated, as the village that it served has also disappeared.

right early in the 14th century although it remained the property of the *See* of Glasgow until the end of the 15th century.

In 1600 the church was *"found altogether fallen to the ground"*, but repairs were delayed until the 1640's while disputes raged over whether or not to move the church to Megget. The present building is relatively unchanged from the 17th century and stands within a picturesque little graveyard. An intricately carved gravestone of 1712 shows Adam and Eve being tempted to eat the fruit of the Tree of Knowledge by Lucifer.

105. Manderston House, Nr. Duns; NT 810 543

The original house dates to the 1790s but much of what can be seen by the visitor dates to the late 19th and early 20th centuries when John Kinross extensively redesigned Manderston, on behalf of the Miller family. The Millers had made their fortune trading hemp and herring with Russia and spared no expense in refurbishing their new home. In addition to the house there are stables, walled gardens, landscaped grounds and an unusual dairy. Open Seasonally. Admission Charge.

106. Maxton Parish Church; NT 610 303

Maxton is an ancient village and there is record of a parish church here in the 12th century, when it was known as St. Cuthbert's Church of *"Mackistun"*. The church was the property of the monks of Dryburgh Abbey from 1326 until the

Reformation. By 1780 the church was in need of repair and it was said to be so cold within that *"none could attend without endangering their health"*. During the course of the next thirty years a slate roof was added, major renovations took place in 1812 and the north aisle was added in 1865. St Cuthbert's Way (**no.142**) passes by the church.

107. *Megget Reservoir, Cramalt Tower; NT 195 227*

In the valley now occupied by Megget Reservoir there once stood two stone towers, possibly connected with medieval gold mining along the Cramalt Burn. The base of one tower has been reconstructed at a picnic site beside the reservoir. This valley formed part of Ettrick Forest and was a favourite hunting site for many of the Scottish monarchs. King James V used the excuse of hunting in the forest as an opportunity to launch punitive raids against the notorious reiving families of the Borders. The reservoir was built in 1983 and supplies Edinburgh with drinking water *via* a conduit tunnelled through the Tweedsmuir Hills.

108. *Meldon Valley, Nr. Peebles; NT 212 429*

Although the Meldon Valley is virtually uninhabited today it contains many former settlements and other archaeological sites dating from the prehistoric period. The valley also contains picnic sites, information on the archaeology and wildlife of the area, parking and toilet facilities.

Both the Black and White Meldons are crowned by Iron Age hillforts, defended agricultural settlements built more than 2,000 years ago. Elsewhere in the valley archaeological excavations have shown that some undefended settlements of round houses date from around 1500 BC, while burial mounds such as the one on

the summit of White Meldon are several centuries older. A wide range of plant and animal life is also present, including the Wheatear, which is a summer visitor to this area.

109. *Mellerstain House, Nr Smailholm; NT 647 390*

Mellerstain House, the home of the Earl and Countess of Haddington, is one of Scotland's finest *Georgian* mansions. Designed and built in stages by William and Robert Adam between 1725 and 1778, it is famous for its ceilings, superb collection of paintings and fine period furniture. The setting of the house includes gardens with attractive parterres and terraces, parkland and a lake. Open seasonally (closed on Saturdays). Admission Charge.

110. *Melrose Abbey; NT 548 341*

Melrose was founded by a colony of Cistercian monks in c.1136. Although this was one of Scotland's wealthiest monasteries, it suffered badly in the wars that ravaged much of the Borders in the medieval period. The magnificent rebuilding of church in the late 14th and early 15th centuries was a result of damage caused by the English in 1385 (**fig.22**). The 16th century Commendator's House is now a museum and the Chapter House contains the burial casket of a heart, thought to be that of King Robert I "The Bruce". In the care of Historic Scotland. Admission Charge.

111. *Melrose, Skirmish Field; NT 533 348*

This area of flat haugh land beside the River Tweed was the scene of a battle in 1526. Sir Walter Scott of Buccleuch brought 600 riders in an unsuccessful bid to rescue the young King James V from the domination of the Earl of Angus and his allies, the Kers and Homes. In the ensuing

Fig. 22 *The rebuilding of Melrose Abbey church in the late 14ᵗʰ/ early 15ᵗʰ century provided abundant opportunities for medieval stonemasons to show off their skills. The sculpture that has survived iconoclasts and weathering includes some of the most outstanding pieces in Scotland.*

combat the Scott faction lost more than eighty men and was routed, although one of Scott's servants, named Elliot cut down Ker of Cessford in the pursuit. The Southern Upland Way footpath crosses the site.

112. Melrose, Trimontium Exhibition, Market Square; NT 547 339

Finds, reconstructions and other information about the 1ˢᵗ - 2ⁿᵈ century AD Roman military complex at *Trimontium* (Newstead) and the native hillfort on Eildon North Hill are presented here. Guided walks around the Roman site are also available in season. Seasonal opening. Admission Charge.

113. Minto Parish Church; NT 566 201

Minto Parish Church is a Victorian building in the *Gothic* style, built in 1830-1. William Playfair, who also designed and laid out the village for the 2ⁿᵈ Earl of Minto, designed the church. An impressive war memorial, by Thomas Clapperton of Galashiels stands to the rear. The church replaces a much earlier medieval building, which stood a short distance to the east and dated back to at least 1275.

Melrose

Origins: *St Aidan of Lindisfarne established a monastery at Old Melrose in the 7th century AD. By 1136 Cistercian monks had established an Abbey on the present site and this became one of the wealthiest monasteries in Scotland. The abbey suffered in the wars with England and closed at the Reformation. The settlement that had grown up outside its walls encroached on the abbey grounds and developed into a market town. In the 19th century Melrose developed into a visitor attraction, and from 1849 the railway brought tourists to the abbey and to Abbotsford, home of Sir Walter Scott.*

Derivation: *Cumbric "Moelros" the bare moor or bare promontory*

Notable Events:

c.AD650: Foundation of Old Melrose by St Aidan.

c.AD859: Destruction of Old Melrose by Kenneth mac Alpin.

1136: Foundation of Melrose Abbey. 1526: Battle of Skirmish Field.

1545: Earl of Hertford's Raid.

1609: Town erected into a Burgh of Barony.

Notable Personages: *Catherine Helen Spence (1825-1910)*

Points of Interest: *Abbey (110), Eildon Hills (47), Melrose Festival (3rd full week in June), Skirmish Field (111), Town Trail, Trimontium Exhibition (112).*

114. Mordington Old Parish Church; NT 946 554

Edgar, king of Scots, gave the Saxon Manor of Mordyngton to the monks of Coldingham in 1098 and the church of St. Mary was constructed after that time. This first church stood in the grounds of Mordington House until 1757, when it mysteriously burned down, and a replacement was built to the north of the Duns - Berwick road where its graveyard can still be seen, just inside the border with England. This second church lasted for only 110 years before it, in turn, was replaced. The new building was built within the present parish graveyard, and continued in use until 1987, when the condition of the roof caused its closure. This third church was demolished in 1989.

115. Newark Castle; NT 420 293

In 1423 the *"New Werk"* of the Earls of Douglas was built to replace an earlier stronghold (the *"Oldworck"*), but they forfeited it to the Crown in mid-15th century. English armies attacked the castle twice in the 16th century and it fell to the forces of Oliver Cromwell in 1650. In the 18th century the castle had its roof removed along with most of the dressed stone facings. The tower still survives to wall walk level, and stands within a 16th century barmkin or courtyard, the wall of which is pierced by numerous gun-loops. The Royal Arms of Scotland are carved into the west gable of the tower and may record a grant of 1473 when King James III gave the Forest of Ettrick to his wife, Margaret of Denmark. In 1645 Royalist prisoners, captured at the Battle of Philiphaugh, were murdered in cold blood at nearby Slain Men's Lea. **The tower is not open to the public and should be viewed from the road.**

116. Newcastleton, Liddesdale Heritage Centre and Museum; NY 481 872

The Museum recounts the story of Liddesdale, once the most notorious lair of reivers in the whole of the Borders. Also of interest is a display of railway memorabilia relating to the Waverley Route, which closed in 1969 and was the only main line railway included in the Beeching cuts.

117. Newcastleton, Planned Village; NY 483 874

The site of Newcastleton was formerly a medieval hamlet known as Copshaw Holm. The Third Duke of Buccleuch founded Newcastleton in 1793 to concentrate the dispersed rural population and develop the weaving industry. Its grid plan was based on two axial streets and by 1800 two hundred and twenty houses had been built, many of them with a large front window to provide maximum light for the weavers. The village is no longer involved in weaving but retains its 19th century character. Walks from the village lead to other points of interest, including Mangerton Tower that was once home to the notorious reiving family of the Armstrongs.

118. Newcastleton, Priest Hill Forest Walk; NY 503 877

Newcastleton Forest still contains stands of trees that date from the 1920s, when the Forestry Commission first planted the east side of the valley. Dykecrofts Information Centre houses an exhibition of forestry past and present and is linked to a series of forest paths. One of these is around Priest Hill and provides opportunities to examine the remains of an Iron Age hillfort, abandoned medieval farmsteads and excellent views of Liddesdale. Additionally, the Cross-Border Cycle Trail from Kielder Water can be joined at Dykecrofts.

119. Newlands Old Parish Church; NT 161 465

In c.1275 the post of *Rector* at Newland was valued at £160 and in the 14th century the church had close links with the monks of Dunfermline Abbey and the collegiate church of Dalkeith. The earliest surviving stonework dates from the first half of the 16th century and the south wall and east end were remodelled in the 18th and 19th centuries. The present parish church was built on a neighbouring site in 1838, but its derelict predecessor continued to receive burials and there are a number of interesting carved gravestones in the churchyard.

120. Newstead, Rhymer's Stone; NT 565 335

The traditional site of the legendary meeting between Thomas the Rhymer of Ercildoun and the Queen of the Fairies is marked by a viewpoint, which overlooks the Tweed valley and stands beside the former road from Melrose to St Boswells.

121. Newstead, Trimontium; NT 571 345

In c.79AD Julius Agricola, Governor of Britain established the first Roman occupation of the Southern Uplands and strengthened his conquests with forts. The site of the most important Roman military complex in southern Scotland is marked by the Trimontium monument, a large inscribed pillar of marble beside the old road from Newstead to Leaderfoot. The Roman fort, annexes and temporary camps have been ploughed level by centuries of cultivation, but viewpoints and information boards assist the visitor to understand the site, which includes the upstanding earthworks of a small amphitheatre. Finds from the site are displayed in the Trimontium Exhibition in Melrose **(no.112)**.

122. North Muir, Nether and Upper Cairns, Nr West Linton; NT 113 512 and NT 110 509

On North Muir are two outstanding examples of prehistoric burial mounds, which date to a period around 2,500 to 2,000 BC. Both cairns are situated close to a footpath and can be viewed from it. The "Nether Cairn" is 3.6m (12ft) in height with what appears to be a "kerb" or platform around it and traces of an enclosing ditch (**fig.23**). The "Upper Cairn" is largely overgrown, but stands to a height of 4.2m (13ft).

123. Paxton House; NT 931 519

Paxton House was built between 1758 and 1766 for Patrick Home of Billie and is one of the finest 18th century *Palladian* country houses in Britain. The house boasts interiors by Robert Adam, furniture by Thomas Chippendale and over 70 paintings from the National Galleries of Scotland. Paxton occupies the site of a fortified bridgehead dating from the First Bishops' War of 1639. The gardens are open to the public and there are pleasant walks beside the Tweed. Open Seasonally. Admission Charge.

124. Pease Dean; NT 791 699

This steep sided valley runs inland from the sea and is home to a rich flora of ancient woodlands with rare orchids and other plants including Soft Shield Fern. A section of the Southern Upland Way runs through semi-natural woodland, which is a protected Scottish Wildlife Trust Reserve. Towering over the dean is the "Pease Bridge" which was reputed to be the highest bridge in Europe at the time of its construction 200 years ago. Pease Mill, a former corn mill stood immediately to the north of the confluence of the Pease and Tower Burns in the 1740s.

Peebles

Origins: The royal castle of Peebles was built on the headland between the Eddleston Water and the River Tweed in the 12th century and dominated the royal burgh as represented by the "Old Town", which extended as far as St Andrew's Church. By the 15th century the burgh had been re-designed and the "New Town" laid out on based on the present High Street. Peebles continued to serve as a County Town (until 1975) and market, but saw limited industrial development.

Derivation: Cumbric "Pebyll" tents or place where the tents are pitched.

Notable Events:

1261: Discovery of an inscribed stone cross leads to foundation of the Cross Kirk.

1474: Trinitarian Order set up at the Cross Kirk.

1549: Town attacked and burnt by English raiders.

1570: Town Wall erected.

1650-1: Town occupied by Cromwell's Troops.

Notable Personages: William Chambers (1800-83), John Veitch (1829-94)

Points of Interest: Beltane Festival (middle of June), Chambers Institution and Tweeddale Museum (**125**), Cross Kirk (**126**), Neidpath Castle (**127**), Neidpath Viaduct (**128**), St Andrew's Church (**129**), Town Trail, Town Wall (**130**).

Fig. 23 *Nether Cairn on North Muir stands almost 4m (13ft) high and is a burial mound erected more than 4,000 years ago. Cairns of such exceptional size may also have been a focus for religious ceremonial.*

125. Peebles, Chambers Institution, High Street; NT 252 404

William Chambers, compiler of Chambers' Dictionary was a native of Peebles and gave the Institution to the Burgh with the purpose of 'social improvement'. It contained a library, reading room, art gallery and museum. Before its extensive remodelling, the Chambers Institution was known as 'Queensberry Lodging' or 'Dean's House' and the central portion of the present building probably dates from the 16th or 17th century. Today it houses the local museum and contains various displays about the history and archaeology of Tweeddale.

126. Peebles Cross Kirk; NT 250 407

The church was built in the late 12th century to mark the site of the discovery of a 'magnificent and venerable cross'. A *Trinitarian* Friary was established on the site in 1474, at which time a cloister and domestic buildings were erected **(fig.24)**. The complex was burnt by the English in 1549 and later restored, only for the friars to be dispersed as a result of the Reformation of 1560. The church was appropriated to serve the parish and the redundant friary buildings were gradually quarried for building materials, some of which were used to construct three burial aisles in the 17th and 18th centuries. The church was abandoned

Fig 24. *The Cross Kirk at Peebles was built to house a religious relic that was found on the site in the late 12th century. In the 15th century a monastic house of Trinitarian Friars was added to the establishment.*

in 1784 on completion of the new parish church and soon fell into disrepair. What may have been the original cross, a boulder inscribed with a cross and inscription to "Neitan the priest" was unearthed from a nearby garden wall in the 1960s and is now in the Museum of Scotland in Edinburgh. In the care of Historic Scotland.

127. Peebles, Neidpath Castle;
NT 236 404

This impressive castle was probably built in the latter part of the 14th century by the Hays of Locherworth to dominate the passage of Tweeddale at Neidpath Gorge. Originally known as the castle of Jedderfield, its present name was adopted during the 16th century. There are no records of any military action around the castle

before the Civil Wars of the 17th century, when the garrison surrendered to the troops of Oliver Cromwell. The castle was subsequently extensively altered and improved, but by 1790 part of the building was ruinous. The poet William Wordsworth deplored the felling of much of the woodland around the castle at about this time. Neidpath is in private ownership and there are seasonal opening times. Admission Charge.

128. Peebles, Neidpath Viaduct;
NT 232 401

This railway bridge is one of the finest examples of *skewed arch* construction in Scotland (**fig.25**). The viaduct was opened on the 1st February 1864, for the Symington, Biggar & Broughton Railway, which was subsequently taken over by the Caledonian Railway. The railway provided an

Fig. 25 Neidpath Viaduct opened in 1864 to carry the Symington, Biggar and Broughton Railway across the Neidpath Gorge. The former railway line still forms part of the Tweed Walk between Peebles and Lyne.

important link to the wider rail network until it's closure in 1954.

129. Peebles, St Andrews Church; NT 244 406

The restored tower and the fragmentary remains of the nave of St Andrew's Church stand within the present graveyard. The original church was founded during in the 12th century and was dedicated by Jocelin, Bishop of Glasgow in 1195. A college of priests served the church for the six

years up to 1549, when it was burnt beyond repair by English soldiers and abandoned. Parishioners moved to the Cross Kirk after the dissolution of the Trinitarian community there. St Andrew's graveyard remained in use, but the building was used as a quarry for stone in the late 16th and 17th centuries. With the exception of the tower, which was restored by Dr Chambers in the 19th century, the church appears now much as it must have been in the late 1700s.

130. Peebles Town Wall; NT 254 406

In 1569 the Burgh Council of Peebles commissioned *"Stene Robesone, baillie"* and *"Thomas Lawder, masone"* to construct a town wall. During it's construction, which took four years, the town council and the community were required to bring two hundred loads of lime every year to help with the construction. When Edinburgh was in the grip of the plague in 1624 special precautions were taken to control entry to the town by strangers. The town wall was repaired and watch was kept on the four town ports from six in the morning till eight at night *"be four men, maisters of thair famelies, and the principall servantis of those that ar wedowis."* By the late 18th century the town wall was no longer required and only portions of it remained. Today, the surviving section consists of a corner tower with gun-loops and two lengths of adjoining wall.

131. Peniel Heugh and the Waterloo Monument; NT 653 263

The extinct volcanic intrusion of Peniel Heugh means "hill-hill-slope" in a combination of Old Welsh, Old English and Old Scandinavian. Its summit is surrounded by a boulder wall, which may date from the 5th or 6th century AD, when the nearby Roman road, Dere Street was an important route for Anglian invaders. The 48m (150ft) tower was raised by the Marquis of Lothian to commemorate the Battle of Waterloo (1815). Peniel Heugh can be accessed by a public footpath from Harestanes Countryside Visitor Centre **(no.64)**. **Please note there is no public access to the tower.**

132. Pennymuir, Roman Marching Camps and Dere Street Roman Road; NT 755 143

Dere Street **(no.36)** crossed the Cheviot Hills into Teviotdale via the Kale Water valley. At Pennymuir the ramparts and entrances of two temporary camps are particularly well preserved. They are a reminder that Roman invasion forces made the journey from Hadrian's Wall on many occasions between the late 1st and 4th centuries AD. The road itself can be followed from Pennymuir to Whitton Edge and consists for much of the way of an embankment with quarry pits on either side.

133. Polwarth Parish Church; NT 749 494

Although an inscribed stone in the south wall claims that there was a church here before AD900, the earliest records are to the church of *"Poulworth"* which was dedicated by David de Bernham, Bishop of St. Andrews on 7 April 1242. This church has since been replaced by the present building, which was erected in 1703 and incorporates an earlier family vault of the Hume family. In 1684 Sir Patrick Hume was implicated in the Rye House Plot to assassinate King Charles II and was forced to flee to Holland with his daughter Grizel, who for weeks had contrived to hide and feed her father in the family vault beneath the church.

134. Preston Old Parish Church; NT 786 570

Preston church was built in the 12th century and belonged to the Bishopric of Dunkeld. Some of this original structure may survive in the east and west gables and part of the south wall. The present ruins show some evidence of rebuilding and alteration in the medieval period and repairs are recorded in 1671. In 1718 Preston was combined with Bunkle parish and the church was no longer required for worship. The churchyard continued to be used for burial, and the church was sub-divided into family burial aisles. The easternmost aisle preserves in its south wall a narrow pointed window and a stone *piscina* for the priest to wash communion vessels. The westernmost aisle is entered through a rebuilt doorway, which incorporates a number of carved stones from the original Norman church.

135. *Preston, Preston Bridge; NT 787 567*

This fine bridge dates from 1770 and was an important element of the Duns to Grantshouse and Dunbar Turnpike, which was opened in the 1840s. It now affords views along the pretty Whiteadder River.

136. *Redeswire Fray, Carter Bar; NT 702 071*

In 1575, a meeting of the Wardens of the Border Marches (medieval administrative areas) at Carter Bar led to a fracas now known as the Redeswire Fray. A dispute between the Wardens escalated when their followers took up arms against each other. The Scots won the day when a group of men from Jedburgh arrived, bolstering the Scottish force and routing the English. A stone in the field to the east of the Border crossing commemorates this event.

137. *Riccarton Junction; NY 539 976*

The remote railway community of Riccarton Junction serviced the railways of upper Liddesdale, where the Border Counties Railway from Hexham joined the Waverley Route between Edinburgh and Carlisle. The community received a blow when the branch line closed in 1958, and its fate was sealed when the Waverley Route closed in 1969. At its height the community had a grocer's shop, a sub-post office, a small schoolroom, a public house (in fact the refreshment room for the station) and even sported a solitary telephone kiosk. Although very little now survives, the former Generator shed has recently been converted into a museum by the

Friends of Riccarton Junction. Variable Opening Times.

In 1963 the Forestry Commission constructed a forest road to Riccarton Junction. Before this the community could only be reached by rail. Access is now solely through forest and is not suitable for most vehicles although pedestrians should have little trouble.

138. *Romannobridge, Cultivation Terraces; NT 162 470*

On the southwest slopes of Penria Hill, near Romannobridge part of the hillside was terraced in the Middle Ages to provide workable cultivation strips and avoid the soil erosion that is typical of steep slopes (**fig.26**). Although there are many examples of this in the Border hills, here the pitch of the slope, and the number and closeness of the terraces, is particularly impressive and gives the appearance of a large staircase ascending the hillside. The terraces are best viewed from the A701 between Mountain Cross and Rommanobridge. **Please note there is no public access to this site.**

139. *St Abbs Head, Coldingham; NT 916 687*

Hard volcanic rocks make up this magnificent headland, which has some of the highest cliffs on the east coast of Scotland and is home to several different species of seabirds (**Plate 1**). Here and in the immediate hinterland are visible traces of human occupation dating back at least 3,000 years. To the south of the Lighthouse is Kirk Hill, which is identified as the site of the 7th century AD monastery where Abbess Aebbe governed a house of monks and nuns within the earthworks of an earlier fort. West of the lighthouse the small headland of Rampart Hall has been defended by a rock-cut ditch and a stone wall, with accommodation provided by a medieval hall, the

Fig. 26 The lengths to which medieval farmers were prepared to go are illustrated by these terraces at Romannobridge, where the steep hillside has been stepped to allow cultivation and prevent the erosion of soil.

walls of which survive as grass-grown banks. Later use of the headland can be seen in the form of cultivation remains, a 19th century golf course and an impressive lighthouse complex. The National Trust for Scotland owns St Abbs Head and there is a visitor centre with car parking and picnic facilities. **Access to the site is via the Visitors Centre.**

140. St Abbs, Village and Harbour; NT 919 672

This charming fishing village is located on the southern side of St Abbs Head and is popular with divers, as the water here is exceptionally clear and rich in sea life. In the 18th century it was known as Coldingham Shore and only developed with the creation of a harbour here in 1831. This is now represented by the inner harbour, which has altered very little from the original design.

141. St Boswells Old Parish Church; NT 606 305

Although the foundations of the 1652 church, as later modified, are all that can be seen of the old parish church (the former St Boswells Free Church in the village now serves the parish), the first church was built here in the 12th century. In 1153 Thomas de Loudonia was granted leave to build a church to St. Mary at *"Lessedewyn"* (Lessudden is the old name for St Boswells). This was on condition that he also provide an altar in honour of St. Margaret the Virgin and a sung mass each week for the souls of his wife Margaret, King David, and all the "faithful departed". Shortly after its foundation the church was granted to the monks of Dryburgh Abbey.

142. St Cuthbert's Way, Melrose to Lindisfarne; NT 548 341 to NT 853 273

This 100km (62.5 mile) cross-border path links Melrose and Lindisfarne, both places which were associated with the 7th century monk, Cuthbert. Part of the walk follows Roman Dere Street, crosses the battlefield of Ancrum Moor and passes Cessford Castle **(nos. 3 & 19)**. Other sites that are situated close to the path are listed below in the "Heritage Routes" section. A guidebook and map are available from Tourist Information Centres and local bookshops.

143. Scott's View, Bemersyde; NT 593 342

This popular viewpoint provides not only a fine panorama of the Eildon Hills and the Tweed Valley, but also looks directly over the site, *"almost enclosed by the winding of the River Tweed,"* of Old Melrose. St Aidan founded a monastery and St Cuthbert was a monk there in the 7th century AD. Nothing of this monastery survives above ground, save for the earthen *vallum* or protective bank that once enclosed the monastic buildings. **Please note that there is no public access to Old Melrose.**

144. Selkirk, Halliwell's House Museum; NT 469 284

Halliwell's Close is an 18th century passage and contains a range of buildings that were an ironmongery from 1828. The ironmongers' home and shop have been faithfully recreated and the museum also tells the story of the Royal Burgh of Selkirk and its development over the centuries. Open Seasonally.

Selkirk

Origins: *The 12th century royal burgh, dominated by a royal castle, was established as the seat of government for the Forest of Selkirk, Ettrick and Traquair and retained its administrative role until 1975. Although the main product of the town in the 18th century was traditionally shoes (so much so that the inhabitants are known as "Souters"), in the early 19th century the valley floor was developed by Galashiels mill owners for the production of textiles.*

Notable Events:

1107-1124: Foundation of Selkirk Castle.

1113: Foundation of Selkirk Abbey (moved to Kelso a decade later).

1297: William Wallace proclaimed Guardian of the Realm at the Kirk 'o' the Forest (Selkirk Old Church).

1301-2: William Wallace captures Selkirk Castle.

1535-6: King James V grants a charter confirming Selkirk as a Royal Burgh. 1645: Battle of Philiphaugh.

1799: Sir Walter Scott appointed (Depute) Sheriff of County of Selkirk.

Notable Personages: *Mungo Park (1771-1806), Tom Scott (1854-1958)*

Points of Interest: *Common Riding (Friday and Saturday following the 2nd Monday in June), Halliwell's House Museum (**144**), Kirk 'o' the Forest (**145**), Market Square & Pant Well (**146**), Mungo Park Statue (**147**), Ring 'O' the Toun (Town Trail), Sir Walter Scott's Courtroom (**148**)*

145. Selkirk, Kirk 'o' the Forest; NT 470 283

According to tradition, it was in the original parish church on this site that *William Wallace* was named "Guardian of the Realm" in 1297 in the aftermath of the Battle of Stirling Bridge. The present ruin dates from 1748 and was replaced by the present parish church, which stands in Ettrick Terrace, in 1860-63. The churchyard contains graves of some of the maternal ancestors of Franklin D Roosevelt, President of the United States.

146. Selkirk, Market Square and Pant Well; NT 469 284

The focal point of any medieval burgh was the market, or mercat place. Here stood the mercat cross where proclamations were made and punishments meted out, the tron or public weigh-beam where goods were checked for weight, and the pant well or public water supply. At Selkirk each commodity was identified with its own market or particular part of the square and medieval records show that that flesh, fish, butter, cheese and salt were traded in this way. In 1898 Peddie and Washington Browne incorporated fragments of the former mercat cross into a new Pant Well, which stands in the middle of this bustling town square.

147. Selkirk, Mungo Park Statue; NT 471 286

Mungo Park (1771-1806) was a pioneer who explored the River Niger and was born at Foulshiels, 6.5km (4 miles) from Selkirk on the A708 road to St Mary's Loch and Moffat. A statue by Andrew Currie, with supporting bronzes of African figures and scenes by Thomas Clapperton was erected in 1859 at the junction of the High Street and Back Row as a monument to his memory. The former house where Mungo served a surgeon's apprenticeship stands on the east side of the junction.

148. Selkirk, Walter Scott's Courtroom; NT 470 284

In his role as Sheriff of Selkirkshire, famous author Sir Walter Scott presided over the Sheriff Court in this building from its construction in 1803 until his death in 1832. Seasonal Opening. Admission Charge.

149. Simprim Old Parish Church; NT 852 454

Only one gable still stands of this church, which may have been that which Hye (Hugh) de Symprinc owned in the reign of King David I (1124 to 1153) and subsequently gave, along with *"a toft* (farmstead), *a croft* (cottage) *and eighteen acres of land"* to Kelso Abbey. The income from the church went to Thor, *Archdeacon* of Lothian and (probably) rector of the parish, who continued to receive the revenues until the end of his life, after which they too became the property of Kelso Abbey.

150. Smailholm Parish Church; NT 648 346

David de Olifard founded Smailholm church in the 12th century, in return for being granted the manor of Smailholm by King David I. This church was subsequently granted to the Benedictine monks of Coldingham Priory. Most of Scotland's medieval churches have been abandoned and demolished since the Reformation of 1560, but Smailholm church has continued in use to the present day, with various reconstructions and modifications. Surviving Norman work in the chancel includes three blocked, round-headed windows, which are set in walls of evenly coursed *ashlar* (**fig.27**).

Fig. 27 *Smailholm church demonstrates the west-east orientation which was standard up to the Reformation. The narrower eastern section contains parts of the original chancel, including tiny Norman window slits, now blocked.*

151. Smailholm Tower; NT 638 346

Smailholm is a monument to the confidence of its Pringle owners, for it is a landmark for miles around and exceeds even Fatlips Castle for its "king of the castle" defiance. It is built from the rugged *basalt* crags on which it stands and which were formed as molten rock poured from the earth's core some 350 million years ago. David Pringle and four sons died at Flodden in 1513 and the tower itself was attacked by the English in 1543 and again in 1546, when the garrison of Wark made off with sixty cattle and four prisoners. The property was sold to the Scotts of Harden in 1645, but they abandoned the tower in favour of nearby Sandyknowe, where Sir Walter Scott stayed in his childhood. In the care of Historic Scotland. Admission Charge.

152. Southdean Old Parish Church; NT 631 091

In 1388 *"Zedon"* church was the scene of an important meeting. It was here that the Scottish nobles lead by the Earl of Douglas planned an invasion of England. An English spy was present in the church, but was recognised and betrayed his own side's preparations. This enabled Douglas to lead his men against the forces of "Hotspur" Percy and victory, at the cost of his own life, at Otterburn. The church was abandoned in 1688 when the roof collapsed. A replacement church was built in neighbouring Chesters in 1690, although this is now also in ruins.

153. *Southern Upland Way; NT 172 233 to NT 774 710*

This 340km (212 miles) long distance coast to coast footpath, from Portpatrick on the west to Cockburnspath on the east, passes many heritage sites *en route*, including Melrose Abbey (**no.110**) and Thirlestane Castle (**no.94**). Other sites which are situated close to the path are listed below in the "Heritage Routes" section. A Guide book and map are available from Tourist Information Centres and local bookshops.

154. *Soutra, Burial Aisle and Medieval Hospital; NT 452 584*

Standing in apparent isolation on Soutra Hill, is a burial aisle of the Pringle family. However, aerial photographs have shown that there was an establishment – a medieval hospital – of considerable size in the area. This hospital was founded by the Augustinian Order and stood beside the Roman Dere Street, fronted by a large gatehouse. Here the poor received alms, the sick were cared for, travellers were given hospitality and fugitives found sanctuary.

Part of the site was excavated in the 1980s, when evidence of herbal remedies and bloodletting was found. Further information is available on-site where there is a viewpoint with information panels.

155. *Soutra, Dere Street; NT 402 580*

A well preserved section of the strategic Roman road, Dere Street can be reached from the B6368 road on Soutra Hill. Long after the Romans had withdrawn from Britain, this remained the principal north-south route for medieval armies, such as the 6th century warriors of the Goddodin and the armies of Edward I in the Wars of Independence. It was used more generally by travellers and pilgrims, to whom the Soutra Hospital (see above) provided shelter. In the care of Historic Scotland.

156. *Stobo Parish Church; NT 182 376*

The church of St Mungo (or Kentigern) dates to the 12th century, when Stobo was the parish church for the whole of upper Tweeddale. The walls of the tower, nave and chancel date from that time, as do two Norman doorways in the nave and two narrow windows in the chancel. The porch, north chapel and larger windows were inserted in the 14th or 15th century and the church contains medieval tomb slabs and other carved stones. The legendary baptism of Merlin Sylvestris by St Mungo took place on a large boulder known as the "altar stone" a few miles to the east and is commemorated in a stained glass window. This Merlin lived in exile in the woods of Upper Tweeddale and was one of the two pseudo-historical figures that were later merged to become Merlin of Arthurian legend. The churchyard also contains the gravestone of a local soldier, John Noble (died 1823) and shows him carrying his musket.

157. *Stow, Bishop's Palace and Old Parish Church; NT 459 445*

The ruins of the late medieval "palace" or manor house of the Bishops of St Andrews stand behind the Old Parish Church. They represent a sturdy block of three-storeys with a garret, although the side walls have now largely gone. Although the parish church of St Mary of Wedale (the valley of the Gala Water) originated in the 12th century, the surviving remains consist of some late medieval walls with 17th and 18th century additions. The church possessed a relic of St Mary and was one of the few places in Scotland that gave rights of sanctuary to fugitives from justice.

158. Stow, Old Bridge; NT 458 444

Built in 1654-55, during the Protectorate of Oliver Cromwell, this bridge of three arches was provided by the Kirk Session to enable the faithful from the west side of Wedale to reach the parish church. It is an early survival of a stone bridge and was built to accommodate a horse and cart, but probably went out of use in the late 18th century after the creation of the Hawick to Edinburgh turnpike. **Please note that there is no public access onto the bridge which may be viewed from the roadside only.**

159. Swinton, Village Green and Market Cross; NT 835 474

The *"village of Suen or Sweyn"*, was the property of a man named Liulf, son of Eadulf until King Edgar (1097-1107) granted it to the monks of St Cuthbert of Coldingham. People of Anglo-Scandinavian descent settled this part of the Borders and the village grew up around a green in a pattern that is common in northern England. The market cross stands on the green and symbolised the commercial status that Swinton once enjoyed as Burgh of Barony. The green doubled as the village football pitch and the cross is still known as "the 12th man of Swinton".

160. Teviothead, Johnny Armstrong's Grave; NT 404 051

John Armstrong of Gilnockie, an infamous reiver fell foul of King James V, who in 1530 descended upon the area with 10,000 men and took many of the most notorious culprits prisoner. Armstrong submitted to the young king, but instead of being severely reprimanded and released, he and several of his followers were summarily hanged and, according to local tradition, buried at this spot.

161. Thornylee Viewpoint, Nr. Innerleithen; NT 403 365

Thornylee Viewpoint is located in a public forest and provides opportunities to explore a particularly scenic part of Tweeddale, with views of Elibank Castle (**Plate 9**). The landscape has changed dramatically over the centuries and the viewpoint is a good a place to appreciate this. A sculpture of Margaret Murray of Elibank, commonly called "Muckle-mou'd" or "big-mouthed" Meg, recalls how suitors passed her by until a handsome Border reiver found himself locked up in her father's dungeon…

162. Traquair House; NT 330 354

Traquair House claims to be the oldest inhabited house in Scotland and the earliest part of the structure is a tower built in c.1492, when James Stewart, uncle to the king was given a charter to the property. The tower was altered and extended during the 16th and 17th centuries, and two wings were added later (**fig.28**). Accommodation includes living quarters, chapel and a functioning brewhouse, while in the tower it is still possible to see the "priest's hole" which provided a concealed refuge in times of religious intolerance. The famous Bear Gates were added in 1745 and closed in 1796 following the death of the 7th Earl's wife and according to local tradition will not be reopened until a Stewart is once more king of Scotland. House and grounds are open to the public.

163. Traquair Parish Church; NT 320 334

In the 6th and 7th centuries AD the lower Tweed was settled by Anglo-Saxons who spoke Old English, but the Tweedsmuir Hills remained part of the British kingdom of Strathclyde where *Cumbric* or Old Welsh continued to be spoken. The old British name "Traquair" is derived from

Fig. 28 *Traquair House originated as a late 15th century tower, now encased in one end of the main building, which was subsequently altered and enlarged to provide a house of comfort and great charm.*

tref Quair and means *"the settlement on the River Quair"*, although it is still sometimes called Kirkbride. The church of St Bride, first recorded in 1116, was part of the diocese of Glasgow, which paid particular honour to saints from western Scotland, Wales and Ireland. The present parish church was built in 1778 and subsequent alterations include the Traquair burial vault and *vestry*, which were added to the north wall in 1914. The Southern Upland Way passes by the church and connects this site via Minchmoor to Yair Bridge **(no.173)**.

164. *Tweedsmuir Parish Church and Covenanter's Grave; NT 100 245*

The parish of Tweedsmuir was created from Drumelzier parish in 1643. The first minister was Alexander Trotter, who ministered without a church for the first four years of his office, received no stipend during his time there and died in 1661, after having been in *"not only a dying condition, but likely to be smothered in a ruinous house"*. A few years later, during the "Killing Times" John Hunter, a covenanter was *"cruelly murdered at Core Head by Col James Douglas and his party for his adherence to the word of God & Scotland's covenanted work of Reformation 1685"*. His gravestone can still be found in the present churchyard **(fig.29)**, as also can a memorial to over thirty men who died during the construction of the Talla Reservoir between 1895-1905.

165. *Tweed's Well, Source of the Tweed; NT 049 146*

The River Tweed rises at Tweed's Well and flows 160km (100 miles) through changing landscapes to the North Sea at Berwick. The story of the river's journey through the Borders and the communities that it links is told in sculpture as part of a viewpoint beside the modern A701 road **(Plate 15)**.

166. *Union Suspension Bridge, Hutton; NT 933 510*

Built by Capt. Sir Samuel Brown in 1819-20, with advice from John Rennie, this was the first large suspension bridge in Britain. Six pairs of swept, wrought iron cables with iron bolt brackets (invented by Capt. Brown) and iron suspenders support the timber deck and span the gap between two enormous red sandstone pylons. The Union Bridge Tollhouse, now a private dwelling, stands on the Scottish bank.

Fig. 29 The grave of John Hunter (murdered 1685) in Tweedsmuir churchyard is a rare relic of the religious persecution known as the "Killing Times".

167. *Wallace's Statue, Bemersyde; NT 591 326*

On the hillside overlooking the Tweed is a colossal statue carved by John Smith from Old Red Sandstone and erected in 1814 in honour of the Scottish patriot William Wallace, who was active in the Borders during the Wars of Independence. The statue forms part of a designed landscape, which was laid out for David Erskine, Earl of Buchan and one-time owner of Dryburgh Abbey in the early 19th century. The statue was restored by the Wallace Trust in 1992 and provides a viewpoint over the River Tweed and Eildon Hills. There is also a path leading to Dryburgh village.

West Linton

Origins: David I granted Lyntun Ruderic or West Linton to John Comyn. Only after the Union of the Crowns did the village develop in response to its position on the drove road from Crieff and Falkirk to London. A burgh of regality from 1631, West Linton was reputed to be the largest sheep and cattle market in Scotland in the early 19th century. A range of minerals was worked locally and attracted the railway in 1865, although this did not lead to significant growth in the town itself.

Notable Personages: James Gifford (17th century)

*Points of Interest: Bronze Age Cemetery Reconstruction (**168**), Gifford Stones (**169**), Roman Road (**170**), Siller Holes (**171**), Whipman Week (1st week in June)*

168. *West Linton, Bronze Age Cemetery Reconstruction; NT 139 518*

An Early Bronze Age cist cemetery has been reconstructed on a small knoll beside the road to West Linton Golf Course. The original site was exposed in 1993 by the waters of a nearby reservoir and consisted of nine stone-lined burial chambers (**Plate 5**). In addition to fragmentary human remains these contained decorated pottery vessels, worked flints and some of the earliest pieces of lead yet found in Britain. Lead occurs naturally at West Linton and the pieces found took the form of beads, which had been combined with shale discs in a necklace for a small child. This site may be reached on one of a network of paths which radiates from the West Linton Village.

169. *West Linton, Gifford Stones; NT 149 518*

Three sculptured stones of c.1660 are built into the wall of Gifford's Stone House in the Main Street (opposite the Raemartin Hotel: **back cover**). These unusual *baroque* carvings are the work of local stonemason, James Gifford and are all that remains his house, which stood on this site. Each stone panel depicts members of the Gifford family, including him (three times), his wife (twice), his first son and six of his "progenetors". Gifford was a Covenanter and fought for his beliefs at Rullion Green in 1666.

170. *West Linton, Roman Road; NT 126 500 to NT 141 521 and NT 142 526 to NT 145 534*

The old coach road from Edinburgh to Biggar followed the foot of the Pentland Hills and passed to the north of West Linton (**fig.30**). This road followed the line of the Roman road that joined Carlisle and the western end of Hadrian's Wall to the defended port at Cramond on the Forth. Where

Fig. 30 *Ditches still mark the sides of a Roman military road in places at West Linton, where it follows the foot of the Pentland Hills on its way from Carlisle to the Firth of Forth.*

the road crossed the Lyne Water there was a small fortlet with traces nearby of temporary camps to accommodate soldiers under canvas.

171. West Linton, Siller Holes, Medieval Mine Workings; NT 145 533

Siller Holes is an area of disturbed hillside, thick with the remains of old bell pits and overlooking a small pond where evidence of medieval lead mining was identified and many fragments of cloth and leather were uncovered in the mid-1990s. Documentary evidence indicates that mining was taking place in the 1590s and makes specific mention of buildings and furnaces for the winning and processing of the lead ore. Knowledge of the existence of metal at Siller Holes may go back to prehistoric times, for lead beads found in a prehistoric grave at West Water Reservoir (**no.168**) may have come from here.

172. Whitrope Toll, north of Newcastleton; NY 509 978

The Duke of Buccleuch founded Newcastleton in 1793 and the new turnpike or toll road was constructed to link the village to Hawick and the rest of Roxburghshire, which lie to the north of the Cheviot watershed. The cost of construction was recouped by levying tolls from travellers and these were collected at the tollhouse. This stood a short distance to the south of Whitropefoot, and its remains now take the form of low foundations, situated on the west side of the B6399.

173. Yair Bridge and Picnic Site; NT 459 324

This part of the Tweed Valley was traditionally the gathering place of Scottish armies before setting out to invade England, and at such a gathering, in 1349, the Black Death claimed its first victims in Scotland. Yair Bridge was built in

1760 to carry a new Selkirk to Edinburgh turnpike across the rocks and rapids of this stretch of river. In 1832 this route was effectively bypassed by the completion of a new turnpike through Galashiels, which by then had developed from a village into an industrial town. From the nearby car park on the west bank of the river, the Southern Upland Way and other public paths provide an opportunity to explore Yair Forest, which is in the ownership of the Forestry Commission.

174. *Yarrow Stone; NT 348 274*

Saint Ninian spread Christianity among the people of the Southern Uplands in the 5th century AD. The Yarrow Stone dates from that time and originally covered a grave. The inscribed face records the burials of two early Christian princes, Nudos and Dumnogenos, sons of Liberalis (**fig.31**). The stone now stands within a small enclosure beside the farm track a short way from the public road.

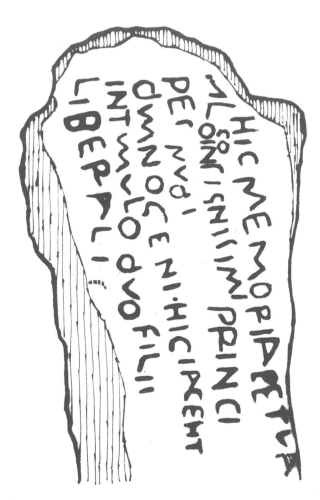

Fig. 31 *According to the Latin inscription, the Yarrow Stone is an early Christian tombstone which once covered the grave of Nudos and Dumnogenos, sons of Liberalis.*

Heritage Routes

Heritage Sites to Visit

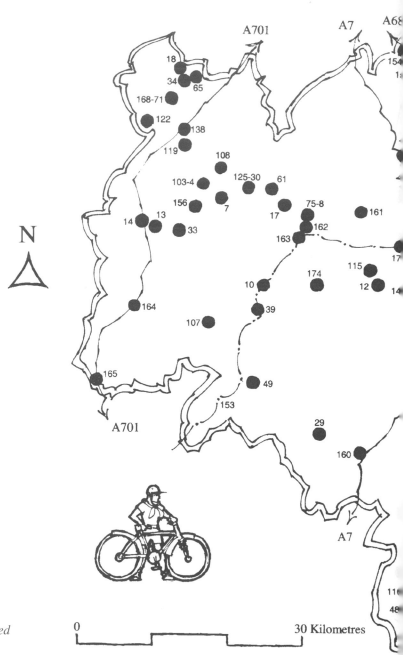

Fig. 32 *Location of sites as numbered in the text.*

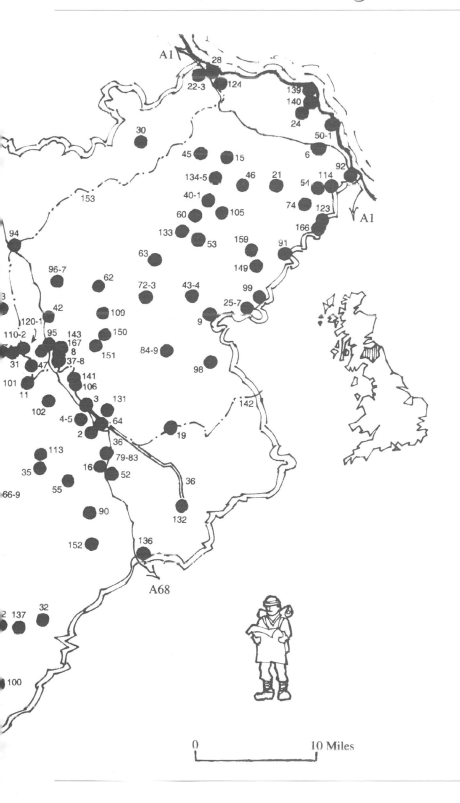

0   10 Miles

Heritage Sites in the Borders

Heritage Routes

Four main roads (A1, A7, A68 and A71) and two recreational paths (Southern Upland Way and St Cuthbert's Way) thread their way through the Borders and provide opportunities to visit some of the sites listed above. The following section provides a summary of those monuments or places that are conveniently placed in relation to these routes.

The A1 East Coast route

A natural routeway across the eastern end of the Lammermuir Hills is provided by the Eye Water valley and the large number of prehistoric burials from here attest the great antiquity of Britain's east coast route. The medieval importance of Coldingham Priory deflected the Great North Road away from the valley and across Coldingham Moor. This was the route used by armies from the time of King John of England in 1216 to Oliver Cromwell in 1650 and was the main land route between Edinburgh and London. Serious efforts to improve the route began in the 17th century, particularly the notoriously difficult passage of Coldingham Moor, but the present route along the Eye through Grantshouse (named after Thomas Grant's Inn) and along the cliffs to avoid Lamberton Moor was not opened as a turnpike until 1810. The constraints imposed my nature also influenced early railway builders, so that the main east coast railway now follows much the same course as the A1 trunk road.

Sites of interest along or within a few miles of this route (from north to south) include:

- Cockburnspath, Market Cross (22)
- Cockburnspath, Parish Church (23)
- Cove Harbour (28)
- Pease Dean (124)
- Southern Upland Way (eastern terminus: (153)
- Coldingham Priory (24)
- St Abbs Harbour and Village (140)
- St Abbs Head (139)
- Eyemouth, Fort Point and Corn Fort (51)
- Eyemouth Museum (50)
- Ayton, Old Parish Church (6)
- Lamberton, Old Parish Church (92)

The A7 Carlisle to Edinburgh route

The Jacobite Rebellion of 1745-46 revealed the shortcomings of the coast to coast routes across the Southern Uplands and northern England. Prior to the 18th century the present A7 route did not exist, although the Roman army had built a road from Eskdale across the Cheviot watershed into Teviotdale. The medieval burgh of Selkirk was linked to Hawick and Carlisle by a turnpike in 1763 and in the following year a second turnpike improved communications between Selkirk and Edinburgh, but did not pass through Galashiels. The modern A7 route was only substantially completed in 1832.

Sites of interest along or within a few miles of this route (from north to south) include:

- Stow, Bishop's Palace (157)
- Stow, Old Bridge (158)
- Galashiels, Englishmen's Sike (56)
- Galashiels, Gala Aisle (57)
- Galashiels, Market Cross (58)
- Galashiels, Old Gala House (59)
- Southern Upland Way (part of: 153)
- Abbotsford House (1)
- Eildon Hills (47)
- Melrose, Skirmish Field (111)
- Melrose Abbey (110)
- St Cuthbert's Way (part of: 142)
- Melrose, Trimontium Exhibition (112)
- Lindean Reservoir (101)
- Selkirk, Halliwell's House Museum (144)
- Selkirk, Kirk 'o' the Forest (145)
- Selkirk, Market Place (146)
- Selkirk, Mungo Park Statue (147)
- Selkirk, Walter Scott's Courtroom (148)
- Hawick, Drumlanrig's Tower (66)
- Hawick, Hornshole Battle Site (67)

- Hawick, Motte (**68**)
- Hawick Museum and Scott Gallery (**69**)
- Teviothead, Johnny Armstrong's Grave (**160**)

The A68 Newcastle to Edinburgh route

The first designed route across the central Borders was built by the Roman army in the late 1st century AD as a rapid means for soldiers to reach the northern outposts of the Empire. Later known as Dere Street, the existence of this road was one reason for the location of medieval monasteries at Jedburgh and Melrose and a castle at Lauder. In the 18th century it was not the redundant Roman road, but the towns which had grown up around these medieval institutions and the physical geography of Lauderdale and Jedwater that influenced the course of the 1768 turnpike between Carfraemill and Carter Bar. Further modifications were made and by 1850 the route was recognisably that of the present A68 trunk road.

Sites of interest along or within a few miles of this route (from north to south) include:

- Soutra Aisle (**154**)
- Dere Street (**155**)
- Channelkirk, Parish Church (**20**)
- Lauder, Thirlestane Castle (**94**)
- Southern Upland Way (**part of: 153**)
- Legerwood, Farm Trail (**96**)
- Legerwood, Parish Church (**97**)
- Earlston (**42**)
- Leaderfoot (**95**)
- Newstead, Rhymer's Stone (**120**)
- Newstead, Trimontium (**121**)
- Eildon Hills (**47**)
- Melrose Abbey (**110**)
- Melrose, Skirmish Field (**111**)
- Melrose, Trimontium Exhibition (**112**)
- Bowden Parish Church (**11**)
- Scott's View (**143**)
- Bemersyde, Standing Stone (**8**)

- Wallace Statue (**167**)
- St Cuthbert's Way (**part of: 142**)
- Dryburgh, Temple of the Muses (**38**)
- Dryburgh Abbey (**37**)
- St Boswells, Old Parish Church (**141**)
- Maxton, Parish Church (**106**)
- Dere Street Walk (**36**)
- Ancrum Moor (**3**)
- Longnewton, Old Parish Church (**102**)
- Harestanes Countryside Visitor Centre (**64**)
- Peniel Heugh (**131**)
- Ancrum, Old Parish Church (**4**)
- Ancrum, Village (**5**)
- Ancrum, Bridge (**2**)
- Jedburgh Abbey (**79**)
- Jedburgh, Castle Jail and Museum (**81**)
- Jedburgh, Greyfriars Garden (**82**)
- Jedburgh, Mary, Queen of Scots Visitor Centre (**83**)
- Capon Tree (**16**)
- Ferniehirst Castle (**52**)
- Redeswire Fray, Carter Bar (**136**)

A701 Moffat to Edinburgh route

Although the Roman road from Carlisle to the Firth of Forth gave rise to the modern A702 through West Linton, the discovery of a sulphur spring in Moffat in 1630 and the development of a spa there led to the development of a more direct route through upper Tweeddale. This enabled wealthy Edinburgh citizens to travel to Moffat and thereby enjoy the waters.

Sites of interest along or within a few miles of this route (from south to north) include:

- Tweed's Well, Source of the Tweed (**165**)
- Tweedsmuir Parish Church (**164**)
- Broughton, Dreva Craig (**13**)
- Broughton, Old Parish Church (**14**)
- Newlands, Old Parish Church (**119**)
- Rommanobridge, Cultivation Terraces (**138**)
- West Linton, Bronze Age Cemetery

Reconstruction (**168**)
- West Linton, Gifford Stones (**169**)
- West Linton, Roman Road (**170**)
- West Linton, Siller Holes (**171**)
- Harlaw Muir, Siting Tower (**65**)

St Cuthbert's Way

The life and times of St Cuthbert inspired this path from Melrose to Lindisfarne. Within Scottish Borders it passes through attractive, rolling country and for some of its length follows the Roman road Dere Street.

Sites of interest along or close to this route (from Melrose to the Border) include:

- Melrose Abbey (**110**)
- Melrose, Trimontium Exhibition (**112**)
- Eildon Hills (**47**)
- Bowden Parish Church (**11**)
- Dryburgh, Temple of the Muses (**38**)
- Dryburgh Abbey (**37**)
- St Boswells, Old Parish Church (**141**)
- Maxton Parish Church (**106**)
- Dere Street Walk (**36**)
- Ancrum Moor (**3**)
- Harestanes Countryside Visitor Centre (**64**)
- Peniel Heugh (**131**)
- Cessford Castle (**19**)

Southern Upland Way

This coast-to-coast path crosses some of the most beautiful country in the South of Scotland on its way from the Dumfries and Galloway boundary to the rugged Berwickshire coast. In its journey through wild upland country it makes use of ancient tracks, such as the Captain's Road and the Minchmoor Road. Elsewhere it runs among trees and woods, beside rivers and through towns.

Sites of interest along this route (from west to east) include:

- Dryhope Tower (**39**)
- Blackhouse Tower (**10**)
- Traquair Parish Church (**163**)
- Traquair House (**162**)
- Yair Bridge and Picnic Site (**173**)
- Galashiels, Old Gala House (**59**)
- Galashiels, Gala Aisle (**57**)
- Galashiels, Market Cross (**58**)
- Galashiels, Englishmen's Sike (**56**)
- Melrose, Skirmish Field (**111**)
- Melrose Abbey (**110**)
- Melrose, Trimontium Exhibition (**112**)
- Eildon Hills (**47**)
- Lauder, Thirlestane Castle (**94**)
- Edin's Hall Broch (**45**)
- Pease Dean (**124**)
- Cove Harbour (**28**)
- Cockburnspath Cross (**22**)
- Cockburnspath Parish Church (**23**)

Further Reading

Further Reading

Ashmore, P J 1996. Neolithic & Bronze Age Scotland. Batsford, London.

Baldwin, J R 1985. Exploring Scotland's Heritage: Lothian and the Borders, HMSO.

Barclay, G 1998. Farmers, Temples and Tombs. Canongate Books, Edinburgh.

Binnie, G A C, 1995. The Churches and Graveyards of Berwickshire. Tweeddale Press, Berwick upon Tweed.

Binnie, G A C, 2001. The Churches and Graveyards of Roxburghshire. Kelso Graphics, Kelso.

Breeze, D J 1996. Roman Scotland. Batsford, London.

Dent, J & McDonald R 1997. Early Settlers in the Borders. Scottish Borders Council, Newtown St Boswells.

Dent, J & McDonald R 1998. Christian Heritage in the Borders. Scottish Borders Council, Newtown St Boswells.

Dent, J & McDonald R 2000. Warfare and Fortifications in the Borders. Scottish Borders Council, Newtown St Boswells.

Dent, J & McDonald R 2001. Farm and Factory: Revolution in the Borders. Scottish Borders Council, Newtown St Boswells.

Fawcett, R 1994. Scottish Abbeys and Priories. Batsford, London.

Finlayson, B 1998. Wild Harvesters. Canongate Books, Edinburgh

Fraser, G M 1971. The Steel Bonnets: the story of the Anglo-Scottish Border Reivers. Pan.

Higham, N J 1993. The Kingdom of Northumbria AD350 - 1100. Alan Sutton, Stroud.

Hingley, R 1998. Settlement and Sacrifice. Canongate Books, Edinburgh.

Lowe, C 1999. Angels, Fools and Tyrants. Canongate Books, Edinburgh.

McAdam, A D, Clarkson E N K, & Stone P 1992. Scottish Borders Geology, an excursion guide. Scottish Academic Press, Edinburgh.

Mackay, J J 1998. Border Highways. John James Mackay, Kelso.

Omand, D (ed.) 1995. The Borders Book. Birlinn Ltd, Edinburgh.

RCAHMCS 1915. An Inventory of Monuments and Constructions in the County of Berwick. HMSO, Edinburgh.

RCAHMS 1956. An Inventory of the Ancient and Historic Monuments of Roxburghshire. HMSO, Edinburgh.

RCAHMS 1957. An Inventory of the Ancient and Historic Monuments of Selkirkshire. HMSO, Edinburgh.

RCAHMS 1967. Peeblesshire; An Inventory of the Ancient Monuments. HMSO, Edinburgh.

Salter, M 1994. The Castles of Lothian and the Borders. Folly, Malvern.

Smout, T C 1969. A History of the Scottish People 1560-1830. Fontana Press, London.

Smout, T C 2000. Nature Contested. Edinburgh University Press, Edinburgh.

Tabraham, C 1997. Scotland's Castles. Batsford, London.

Traquair, P 1998. Freedom's Sword Scotland's Wars of Independence. Harper Collins, London.

Whyte, I 1990. Edinburgh & the Borders, Landscape Heritage. David & Charles, London.

Glossary

Glossary

Angli: the Germanic people who, during the decline of the Roman Empire, settled southern and eastern Britain, which became known as England (Angle-land).

apse: semi-circular or polygonal projection from a building.

archdeacon: a dignitary in the Catholic Church under a bishop who supervised the whole or part of a diocese.

ashlar: squared, dressed freestone block.

Augustinian: Order of canons who followed the Rule of St Augustine of Hippo (AD354 - 430).

baroque: elaborate decorative style developed in 17th century Italy.

basalt: rock formed from lava extrusions.

Benedictine: monastic order established by Benedict of Nursia (died c.AD547).

Bernicia: Anglian Kingdom which extended approximately from Hadrian's Wall to the Firth of Forth.

bishopric: a medieval ecclesiastical province, presided over by a bishop.

broch: defensible stone tower, found only in Scotland, and based upon the traditional round house form. Most were built between the 2nd century BC and 2nd century AD.

Bronze Age: phase of society which followed the introduction of metal working in about 2,500-2,000BC and which lasted until the introduction of iron working in about 700BC.

Burgh of Barony: town endowed with trading rights and administrative powers by an aristocratic (as opposed to royal) proprietor.

chancel: that part of a church reserved for the officiating priest and the altar.

cist: a small burial chamber to contain a single body, and usually made of stone slabs.

Cistercian: monastic Order established c.1098 at Cîteaux (Cistercium) in Burgundy.

Commendator: initially a cleric appointed to administer a benefice for which he was not qualified, e.g. a bishop in charge of a monastery. The practice was extended in the 16th century to enable laymen to draw revenue without performing religious duties.

corbel: projecting stone blocks which support beams or other features.

Covenanter: originally a Presbyterian supporter of the National Covenant of 1638. Extreme elements were persecuted in the 1670s/ 80s for holding open air "conventicles".

conventicle: open air church service held in defiance of Government prohibition.

Cumbric: language of mainland Britain in late prehistoric times, precursor to modern Welsh.

Dalriada: Irish kingdom which included parts of Argyll and the Western Isles in the Early Christian period.

Early Historic Period: the period between the end of Roman Britain and the establishment of stable Christian kingdoms. Also known as the Dark Ages.

Franciscan: Order of friars established by St Francis of Assisi in 1209.

freestone: stone which can be worked in any direction, as opposed to greywacke or whin.

Georgian: belonging to the reigns of Kings George I to IV (1714-1830).

Gododdin: a people known to the Romans as the Votadini, who were the subject of a British epic poem in which a band of warriors ride from Din Eiddyn (Edinburgh) to Catraeth (Catterick).

Gothic: architectural style, developed in France and dominant in later medieval western Europe, particularly associated with the pointed arch.

Gothic Revival: late 18th/19th century style which looked to the later middle ages, not the classical world, for inspiration.

gun-loop: splayed opening in a wall for guns to fire through.

hillfort: type of fortified site occupying a prominent topographical position, and characteristic of Iron Age settlements.

hut circle: remains of a prehistoric roundhouse.

Iron Age: phase of society following the introduction of iron technology around 700BC, generally seen as ending with Roman conquest, but effectively continuing in areas outside the Roman Province.

laird: the landlord of an estate, often equated with the English squire.

merk: old unit of currency.

Middle Ages: the period between the Roman Empire and the Renaissance.

Montrose, Marquis of: Scottish Royalist General defeated by David Leslie's covenanting forces at the Battle of Philiphaugh in 1645.

mort-safe: iron frame or grid placed over grave in graveyard as protection against body snatchers or "resurrectionists".

motte & bailey: earthwork castle consisting of an earth mound (motte) supporting a wooden tower with an adjacent courtyard surrounded by a ditch and palisade (bailey).

nave: the body of a church used by the congregation.

Neolithic: literally "New Stone Age", the period which saw the introduction of farming c.4,000BC. Adoption of metal-working in c.2,500-2,000BC heralded the end of dependence on stone for everyday tools.

Norman (Architectural): see Romanesque.

Northumbria: land north of the River Humber, over which Aethelfrith of Bernicia established his dominion in the early 7th century AD.

Palladian: style of architecture named after Andrea Palladio, whose designs were inspired by ancient Greek and Roman buildings.

piscina: a stone sink for washing the Mass or Communion vessels.

Premonstratensian: Order of canons founded c.1120 by Norbert at Premontré in France.

Reformation: religious revolution, which in Scotland occurred in 1560 and resulted in multiple approaches to the Christian faith at the expense of Roman Catholicism.

reiver: member of frontier society who engaged in kidnapping, rustling, extortion, burglary and/or murder as a way of life.

rector: priest appointed to a medieval parish, and in receipt of the teinds, but often absent.

Rob Roy: Rob Roy MacGregor (1671-1734), Highland outlaw famed for many legendary escapades.

Romanesque: also known as Norman; architectural style popular AD900 to 1150 characterised by round-headed arches and barrel vaults.

Scotti: an Irish people who conquered the natives of North Britain, and imposed their name on the land.

See: ecclesiastical administrative area under the jurisdiction of a bishop.

skewed arch: arch built at an oblique angle to the structure it supports.

Strathclyde: a British kingdom which occupied the Clyde valley in the Early Historic Period.

teind: one tenth part of annual income or produce, equivalent to English tithes, which was due to the parish priest for his maintenance.

Tironensian: monastic Order established at the Abbey of Tiron in Normandy in 1109.

transept: transverse portion of a cross-shaped church.

Trinitarian: Order of regular canons, known as the "Red Friars", established to assist travellers and ransom captives held by non-Christians.

Turnpike: improved road, the cost of which was recovered from tolls.

Victorian: pertaining to the reign of Queen Victoria (1837-1901).

vestry: dressing room for a priest.

William Wallace: Scottish patriot who led the war of Scottish independence against King Edward I of England.

Index

Index

Field Notes

LOCAL COLLECTION